I0763121

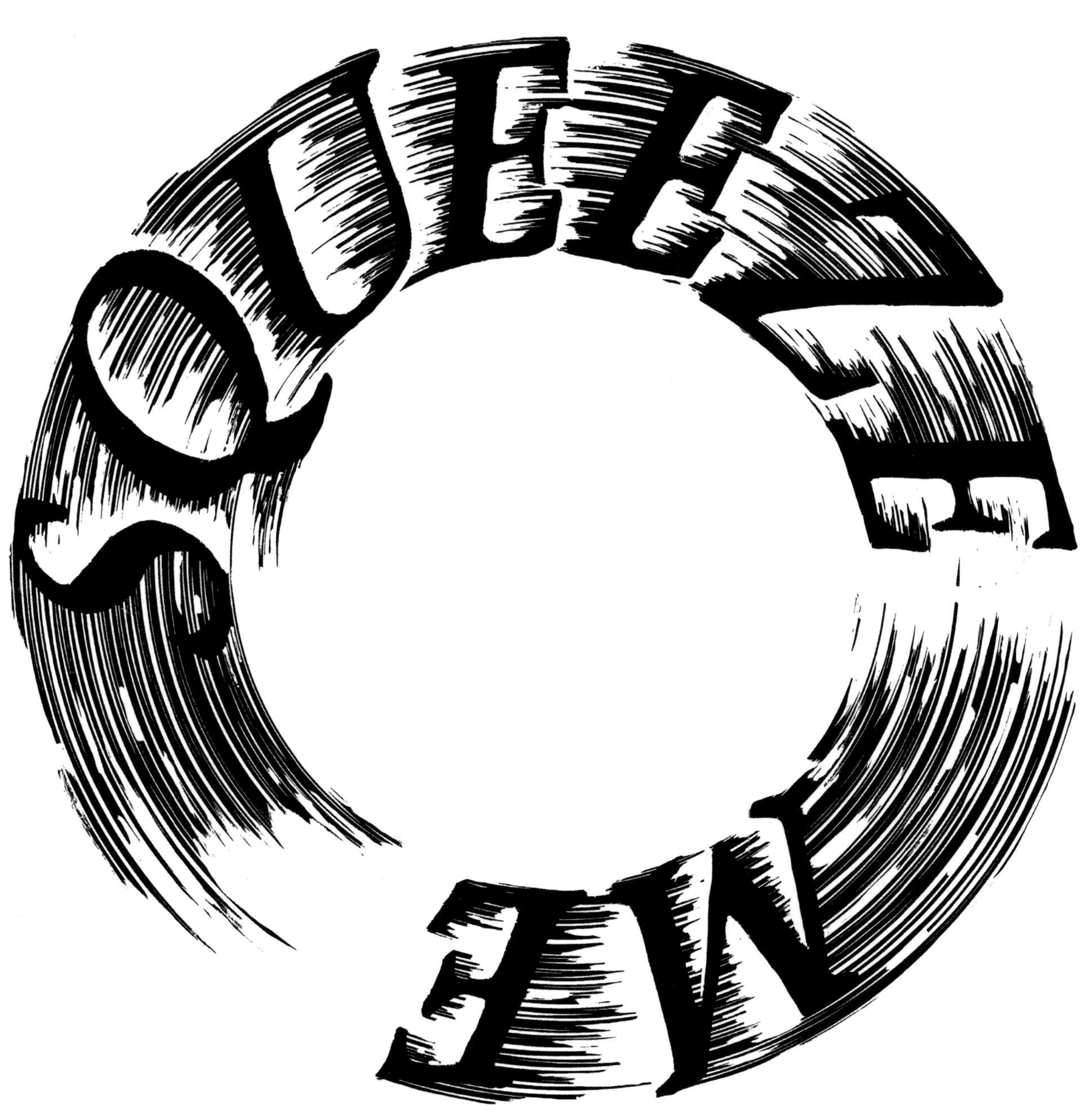
SQUEEZE ME

SQUEEZE ME

Lemon Recipes & Art

Ruthie Rogers & Ed Ruscha

With Heather Ive & Susan Haller
Designed by LoveFrom

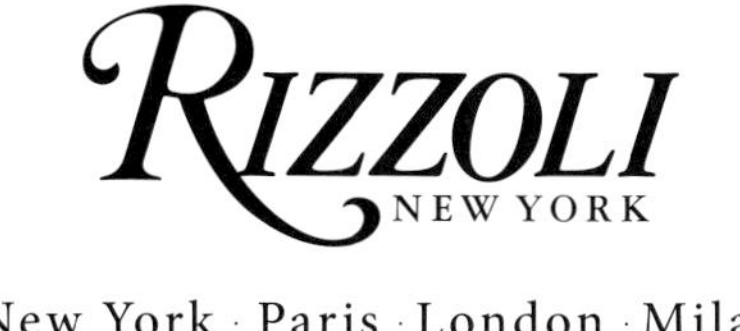

New York · Paris · London · Milan

Two friends, an artist and a cook,
we have wanted to make a book
together for a long time.

Last year,
walking through the lemon trees in
the garden at the back of Ed's studio
in Culver City, we were inspired.
"Let's do a book about lemons."

Lemons are a singular source in cooking.
Sweet in a savory dish,
saltily sour in a sweet dish,
a spice or an herb as much as a fruit.
The rind might be shaved into a whiskey sour,
grated like Parmesan over pasta.

Lemons differ from each other.
Thick-skinned Femminello from Sicily,
large and sweet Cedro from Amalfi,
thin-skinned golden Meyer from California.

This book is a collaboration.
Art by Ed Ruscha;
words by Heather Ive;
design by Jony Ive and LoveFrom;
recipes from The River Cafe;
photographs from Ed's studio by Susan Haller.

Lemons & art,
lemons & friendship,
lemons & books,
lemons & Italy,
lemons & Los Angeles,
lemons & lemons.

Squeeze me.

Ruthie Rogers & Ed Ruscha

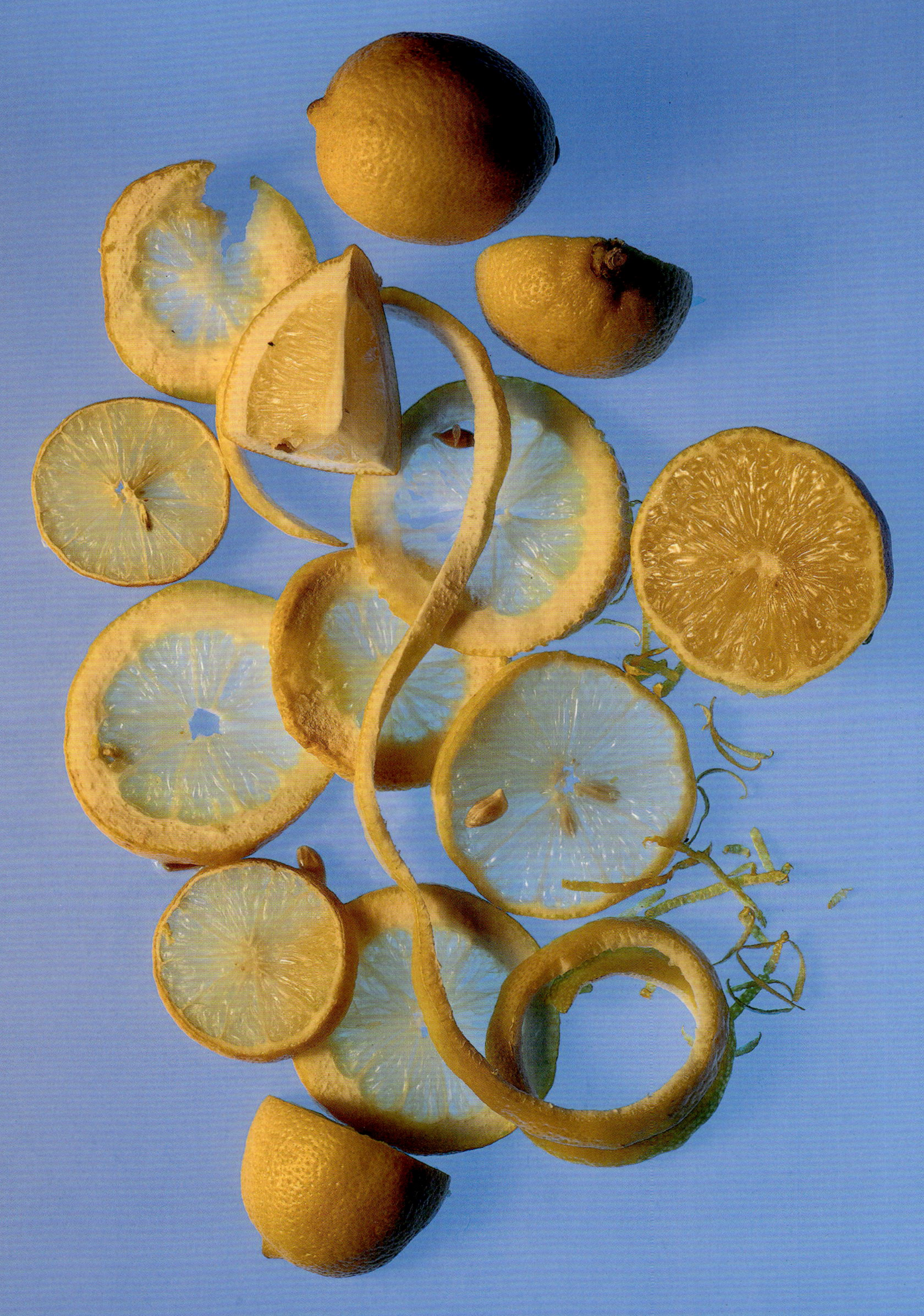
WHEN YOU THOUGHT EVERYTHING WOULD BE
EASY PEASY LEMON SQUEEZY,
BUT IT'S ACTUALLY DIFFICULT DIFFICULT
LEMON DIFFICULT.

Aioli with lemon

- 2 egg yolks
- 1 garlic clove, peeled
- 2 cups plus 2 tablespoons extra virgin olive oil
- Juice of 2 lemons
- Sea salt and freshly ground black pepper

Combine egg yolks and garlic in mortar. Use pestle to crush and stir, blending them together and grinding garlic to very fine paste.

Add oil, drip by drip, stirring all the time. When you have added half the oil, and the mixture is very thick and sticky, thin with a little lemon juice.

Continue to add oil gradually until perfect emulsion forms.

Add more lemon juice, and season to taste.

"LOOK SCOTT,'" I SAID. "YOU'RE PERFECTLY O.K. IF YOU WANT TO DO THE BEST THING TO KEEP FROM CATCHING A COLD, JUST STAY IN BED AND I'LL ORDER US EACH A LEMONADE AND A WHISKEY AND YOU TAKE AN ASPIRIN WITH YOURS AND YOU'LL FEEL FINE AND WON'T EVEN GET A COLD IN YOUR HEAD."

ERNEST HEMINGWAY TO
F. SCOTT FITZGERALD IN
A MOVEABLE FEAST

Bass in the bag with lemon and fennel

- 1 (4½-pound) sea bass, scaled, filleted, and pinboned
- 2 fennel bulbs
- 1¾ sticks/14 tablespoons unsalted butter, softened
- Zest and juice of 2 lemons, plus lemon wedges for serving
- 2 dried chilies, ground
- ⅔ cup extra dry vermouth

Cut each fillet in half to make 4 portions.

Preheat oven to 400°.

Remove tough outer stalks and leaves of fennel. Slice fennel lengthways, keeping green tops.

Blanch fennel in boiling salted water for 4 minutes. Drain and cool.

To make bags, cut foil into 4 × 20-inch lengths. Fold over into 10-inch squares. Smear each generously with butter, leaving half the butter for later. Season with salt and pepper.

Place portion of fish on top half of buttered foil, and cover with a few slices fennel. Scatter with dried chili, lemon zest, and a little fennel herb. Place knob of butter on fish. Bring foil over fish, and fold to seal each side, leaving the top open. Pour a little vermouth and lemon juice into each, then seal top edge. Repeat for remaining fish portions.

Place bags on tray into preheated oven. Bake 15 minutes or until bags inflate. Split open each bag and serve with additional lemon wedges.

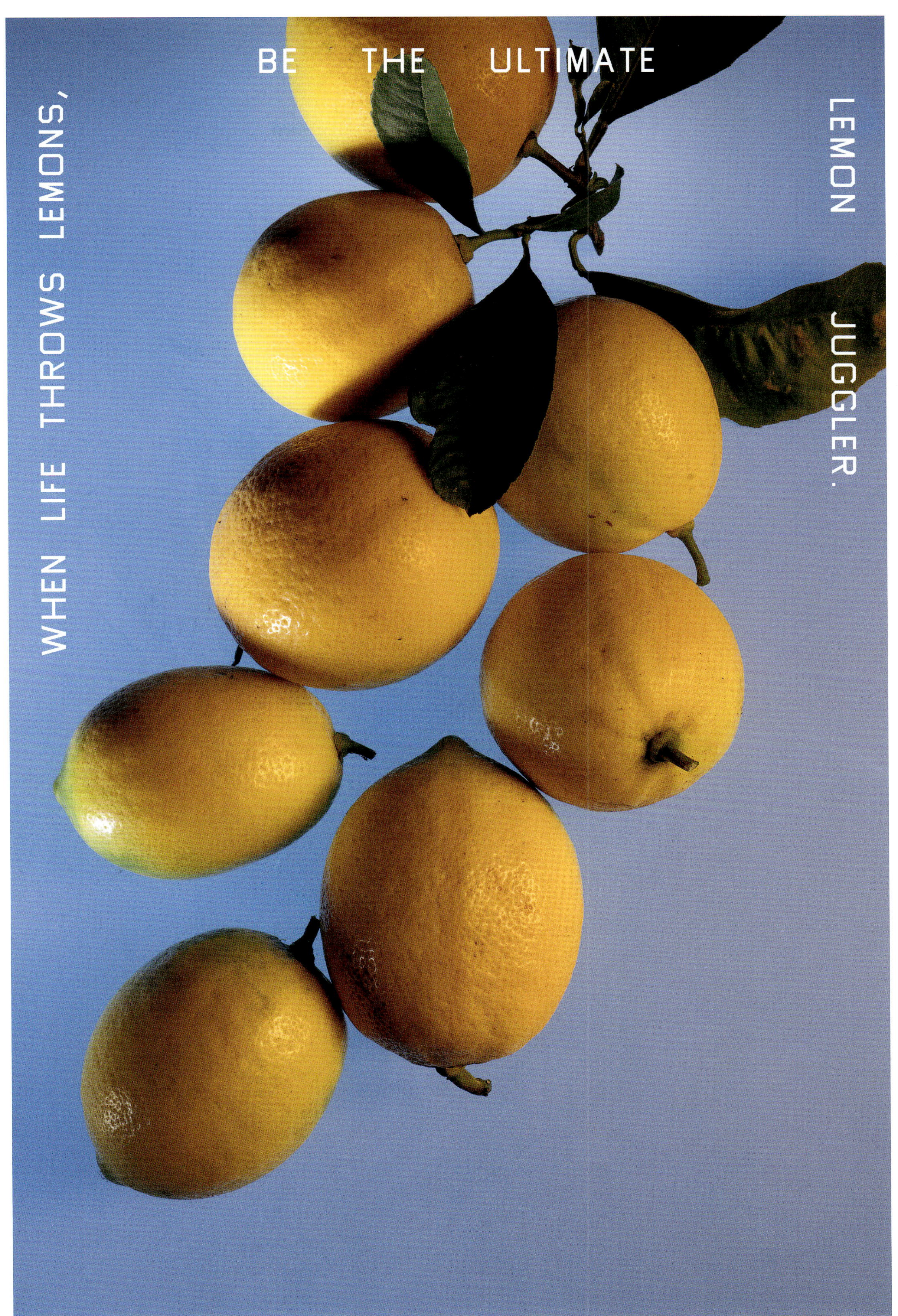
WHEN LIFE THROWS LEMONS,
BE THE ULTIMATE
LEMON JUGGLER.

TO POWER A FLASHLIGHT

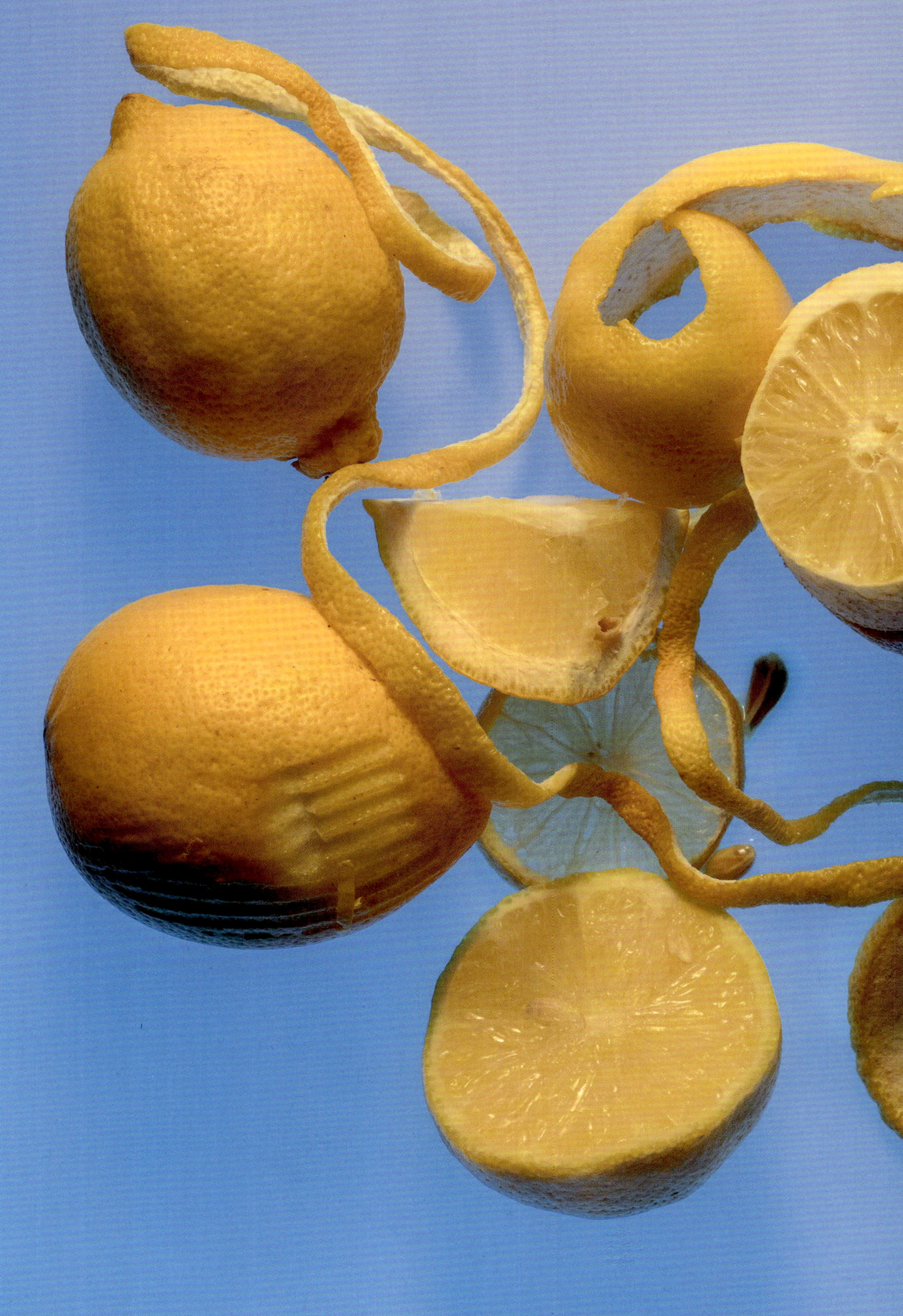

TO CONDUCT

ELECTRICITY.

BULB , YOU NEED A

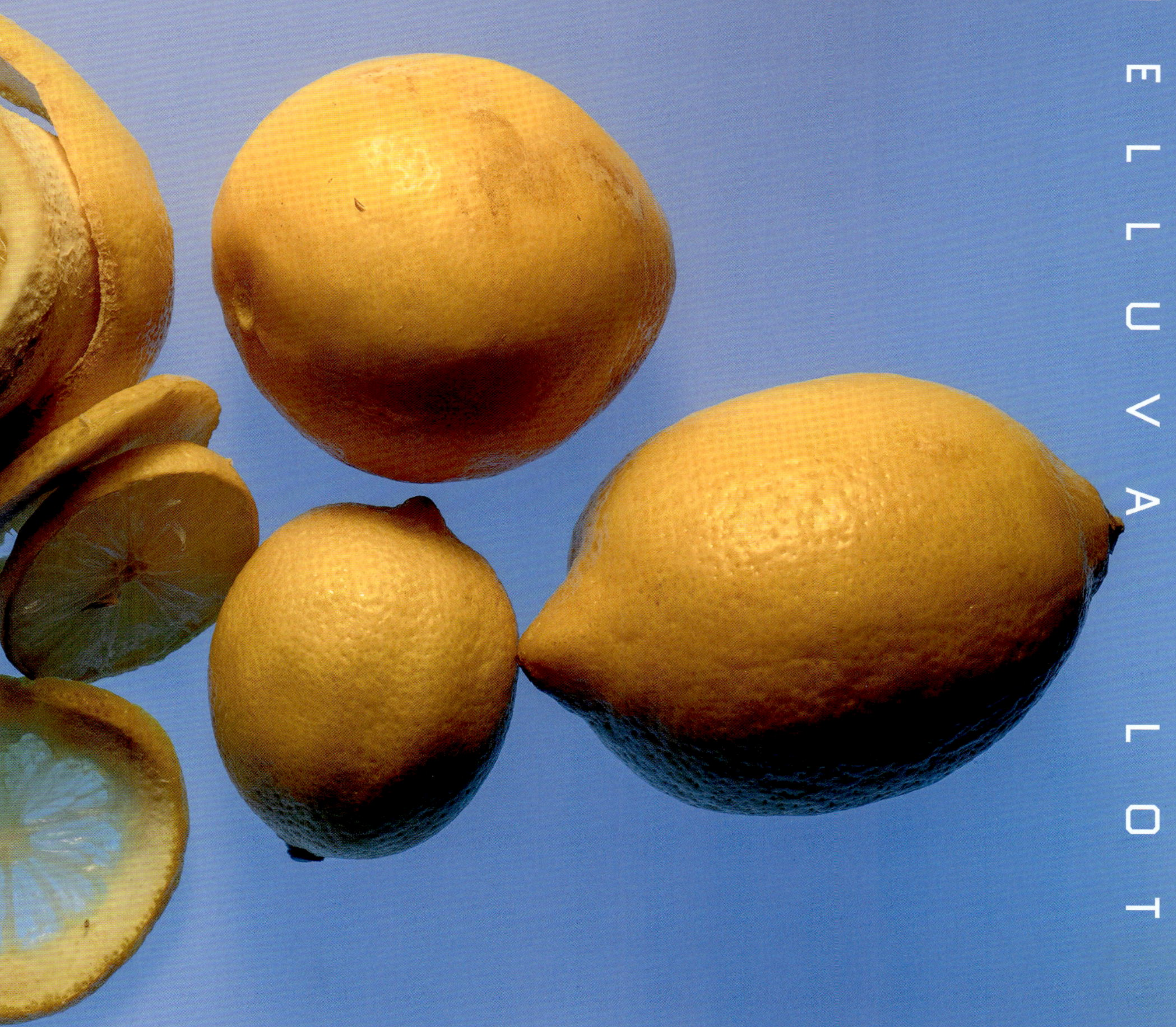

HELLUVA LOT

OF WIRED LEMONS

Bitter greens salad with lemon and capers

- 3 large lemons
- ¼ cup salted capers, prepared
- 1 small dried red chili
- Leaves of 1 small bunch thyme
- 1 pound Catalogna chicory, trevise, grumolo verde, dandelion, or radicchio
- Juice of 2 Seville oranges

Slice lemons crosswise as finely as possible. Cut away only the yellow peel, leaving a little white pith, and remove any seeds. Lay slices out on a flat plate, season with salt and pepper, and drizzle with olive oil.

Combine dried chili, capers, thyme leaves, and 3 tablespoons olive oil. Scatter over sliced lemon.

Remove any damaged outer leaves from grumolo verde, and break open the hearts. Use only the tender hearts of chicory, dandelion and trevise. Wash and dry well.

Mix orange juice with equal amount olive oil. Season to taste. Toss leaves with this dressing, then place dressed leaves over the lemon slices. Serve.

SHE WAS BITTER AND TWISTED AND

IT DROVE A WEDGE

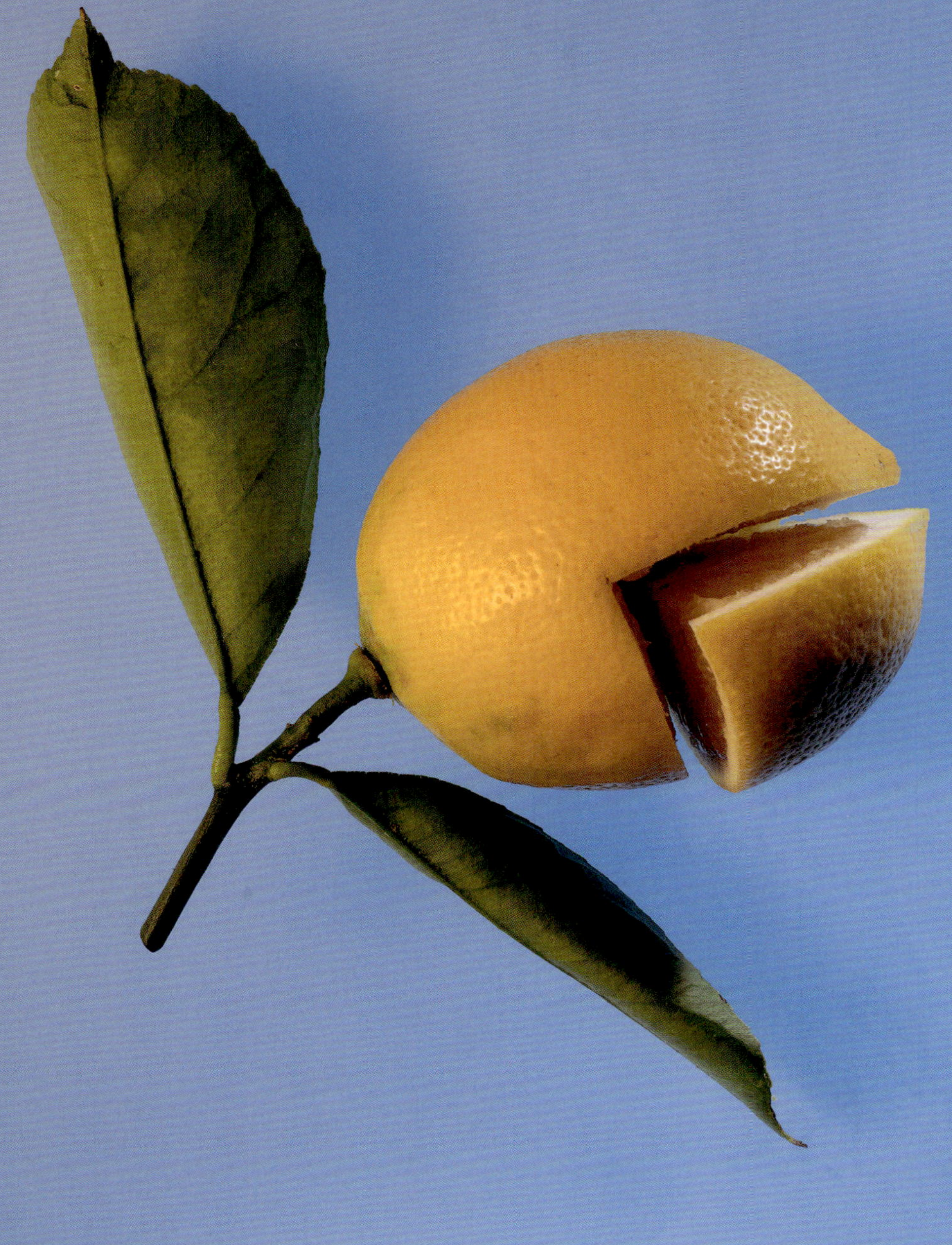

BETWEEN THEM.

I CLING TO YOU

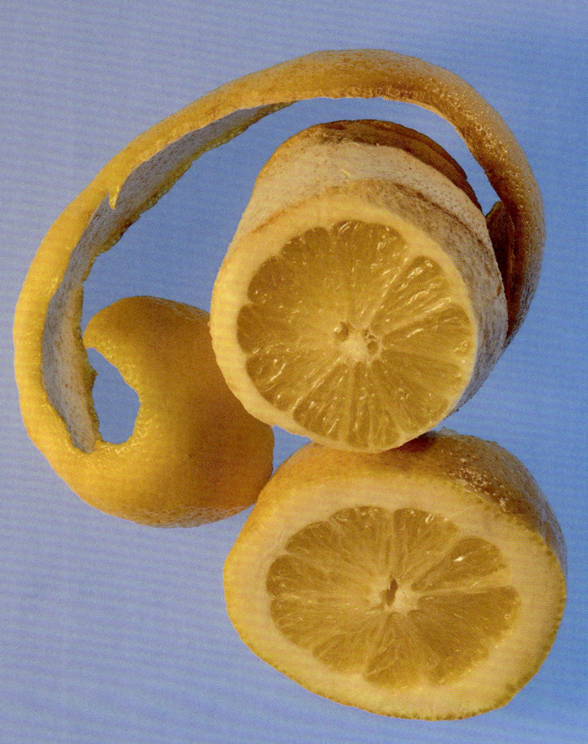

(SAID THE PITH TO THE RIND)

Candied lemon and orange peel

- 1 orange, washed
- 2 thick-skinned leafy lemons or 1 cedro lemon, washed
- 1 teaspoon sea salt
- 4¾ cups superfine sugar

Cut whole fruits into quarters or eighths if large. Remove peel from flesh, keeping porous white pith attached to peel, and scrape off any membrane to expose pith.

Place peel into large pan and cover with cold water. Add 1 teaspoon salt, bring to boil, then drain. Return peel to empty pan, cover with fresh cold water, bring to boil for further 5 minutes, then drain again. Repeat process 4 or 5 times, until peel is tender and has lost bitter taste.

Combine sugar in pan with 1 cup cold water. Slowly bring to boil until sugar dissolves, then turn heat down. Add washed lemon leaves and simmer for 10 minutes.

Add the peel—it should be covered by the syrup—and continue to simmer for 45 minutes, or until peel is translucent. Drain peel and cool on waxed parchment paper. Serve or store in sterilized airtight jar for up to 3 months.

Cedro lemon and celery salad

- 1 large cedro lemon, washed
- 2 heads celery, inner white hearts and leaves only
- 2 large, fresh red chilies
- Juice of 1 lemon
- 5 ounces rocket leaves

Peel off any discolored or rough parts of the cedro skin. Slice cedro lemon very finely.

Slice celery hearts at an angle, and chop celery leaves. Cut chilies in half lengthways, remove seeds, and thinly slice.

Mix sliced cedro and celery together in a bowl. Add chopped celery leaves and chili, and season generously with salt and pepper. Pour over lemon juice, drizzle with olive oil, and toss with undressed rocket leaves.

I WAS ABSOLUTELY TAKEN BY THAT LEMON. THE COLOR, PURE AND SIMPLE, LIKE LEMON YELLOW PIGMENT STRAIGHT OUT OF THE TUBE, SOLIDIFIED. AND PERFECTLY SHAPED LIKE A SQUAT WEAVING SPINDLE.

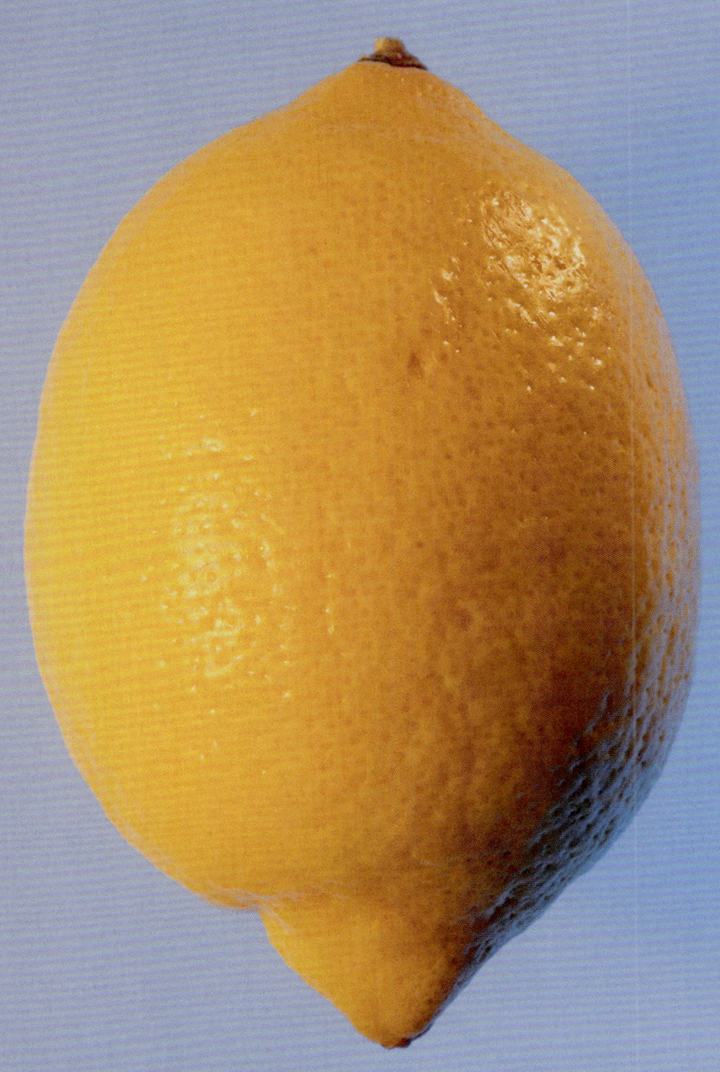

FROM "LEMON," AN ESSAY BY KAJII MOTOJIRO

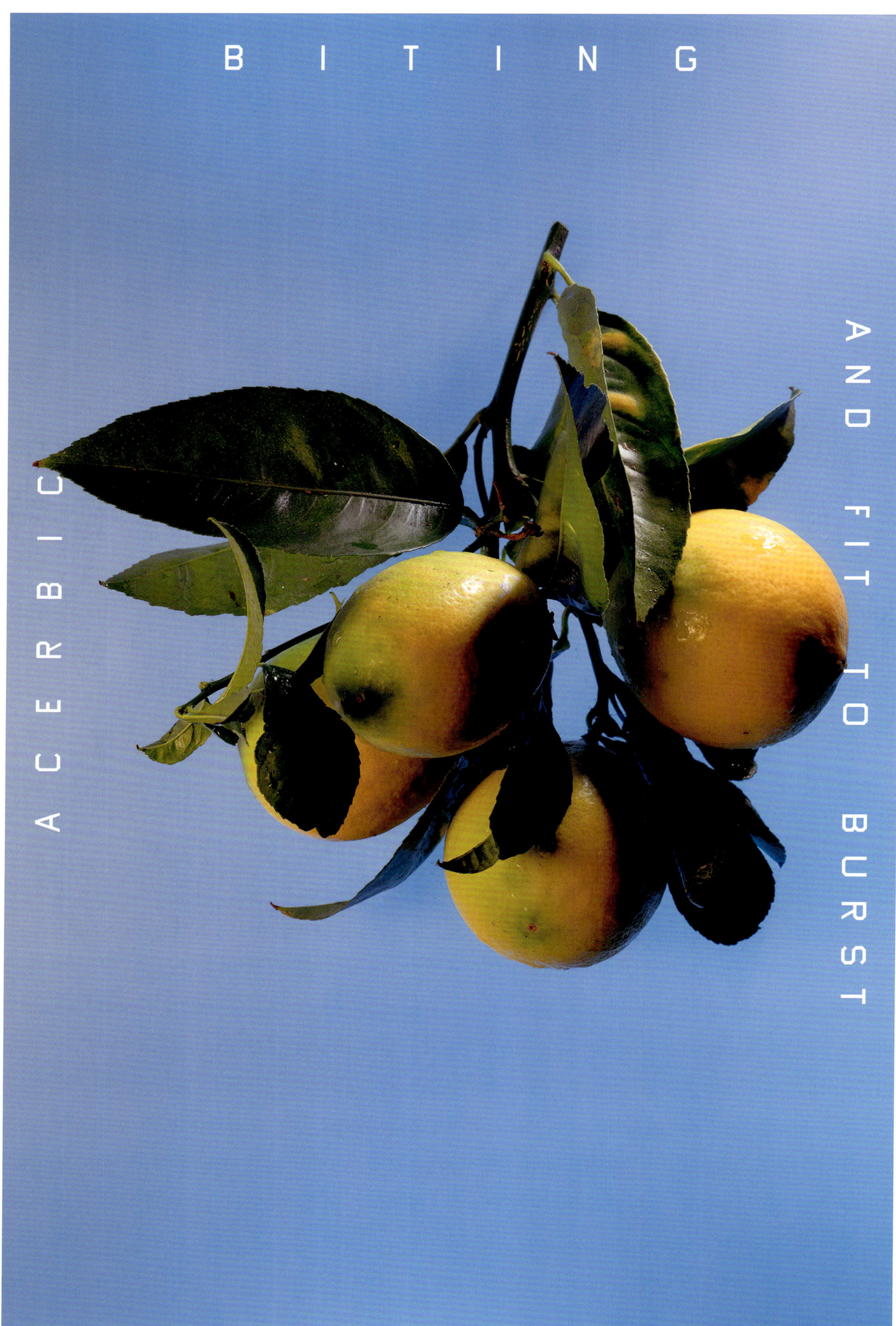
BITING
ACERBIC
AND FIT TO BURST

Flattened chicken with lemon

- 3 to 3½ pound organic whole chicken, deboned
- 4 cloves garlic, finely chopped
- 3 tablespoons chopped thyme leaves
- 1 tablespoon sea salt, plus more for seasoning
- Freshly ground black pepper
- Olive oil
- 2 lemons, juiced
- 1 lemon cut into wedges for serving

Preheat oven to 425°.

Lay chicken on chopping board with skin facing down. Using your finger, gently prise skin away from meat to create pockets.

Finely chop garlic with thyme, adding 1 tablespoon salt. Push this mixture into chicken flesh and pockets, then scatter remainder over surface. Season with salt and pepper.

Drizzle oven tray with olive oil. Lay chicken with skin facing up, squeeze over the juice of 1 lemon, and drizzle with olive oil. Roast 30–40 minutes, basting occasionally with juices from pan and remaining lemon juice.

Carve by cutting across the chicken in thick slices. Serve with lemon wedges.

Green chili and lemon peel sauce

- 6 hot green chilies
- Peel of 1 lemon
- Sea salt and freshly ground black pepper
- Extra virgin olive oil

Seed and finely chop chilies.

Slice lemon peel into very fine strips. Combine with chopped chili. Add salt and pepper to taste, and mix with olive oil to cover. Let sit for several hours before serving.

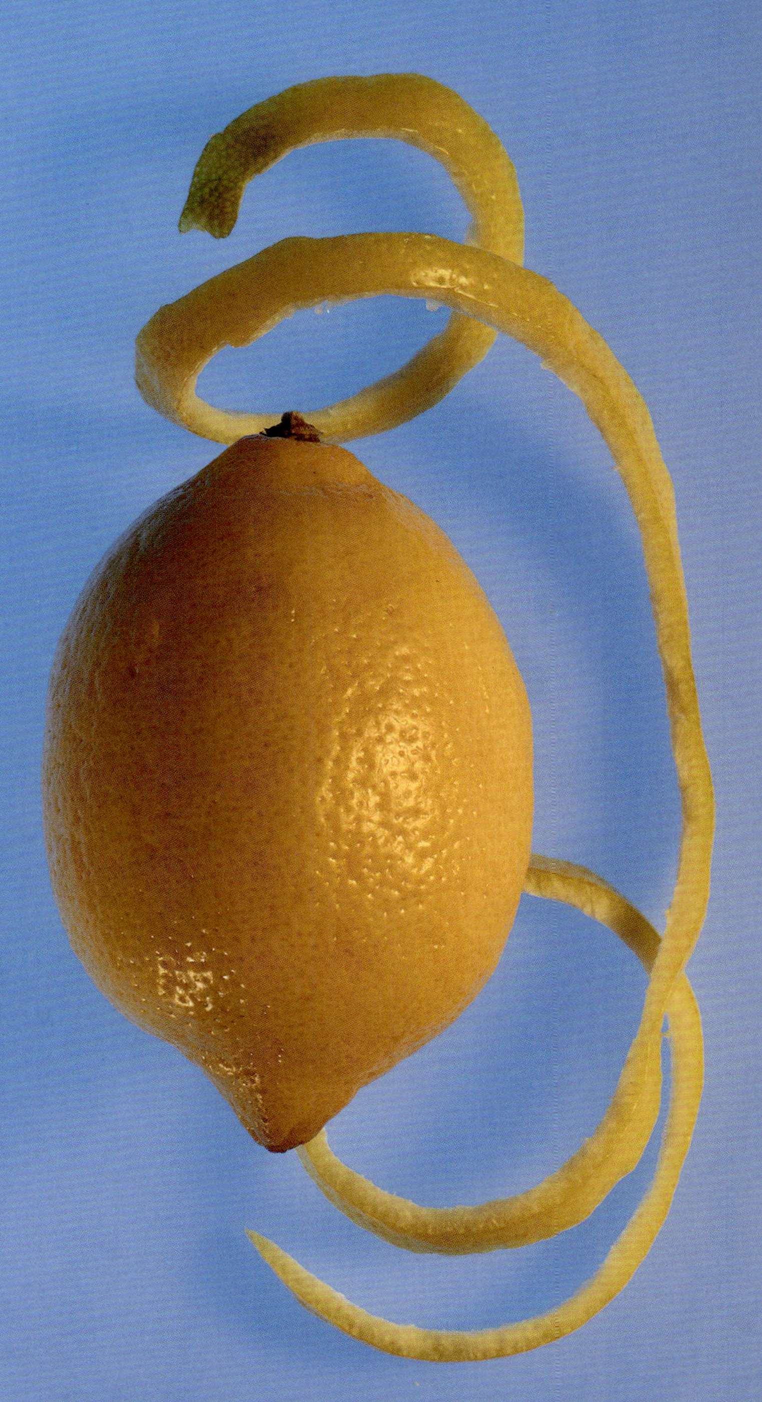

I KNOW SOUR,
WHICH ALLOWS ME
TO APPRECIATE THE SWEET.

YOU GOTSTA KILL SOME LEMONS IF YOU WANTS SOME LEMONADE.

LI'L ABNER

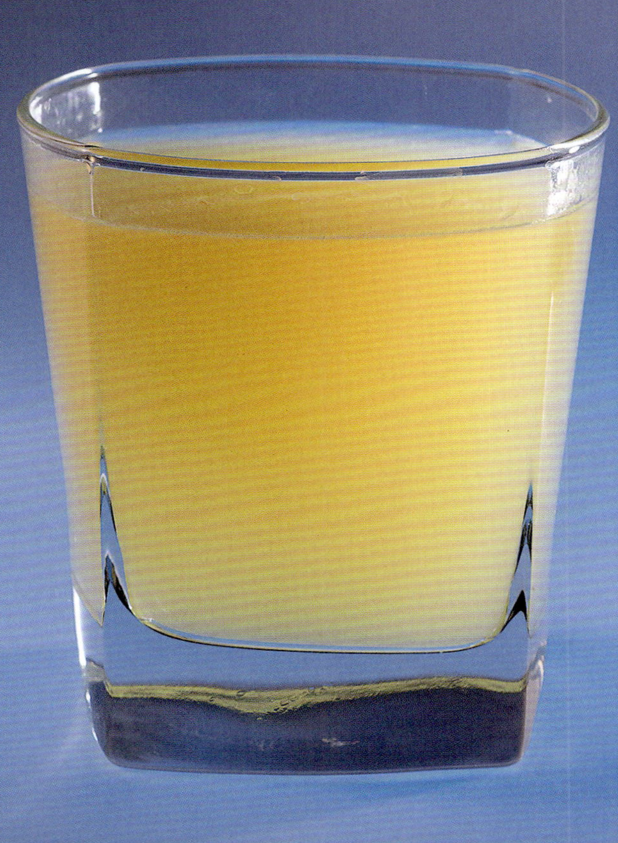

Lemonade

- ½ cup sugar
- Juice of 12 lemons

Combine sugar with 5 ounces water in small saucepan. Bring to simmer, stirring occasionally, until sugar is dissolved. Cool completely.

In large pitcher, combine 2½ cups water with lemon juice and cooled syrup. Serve over cubed ice.

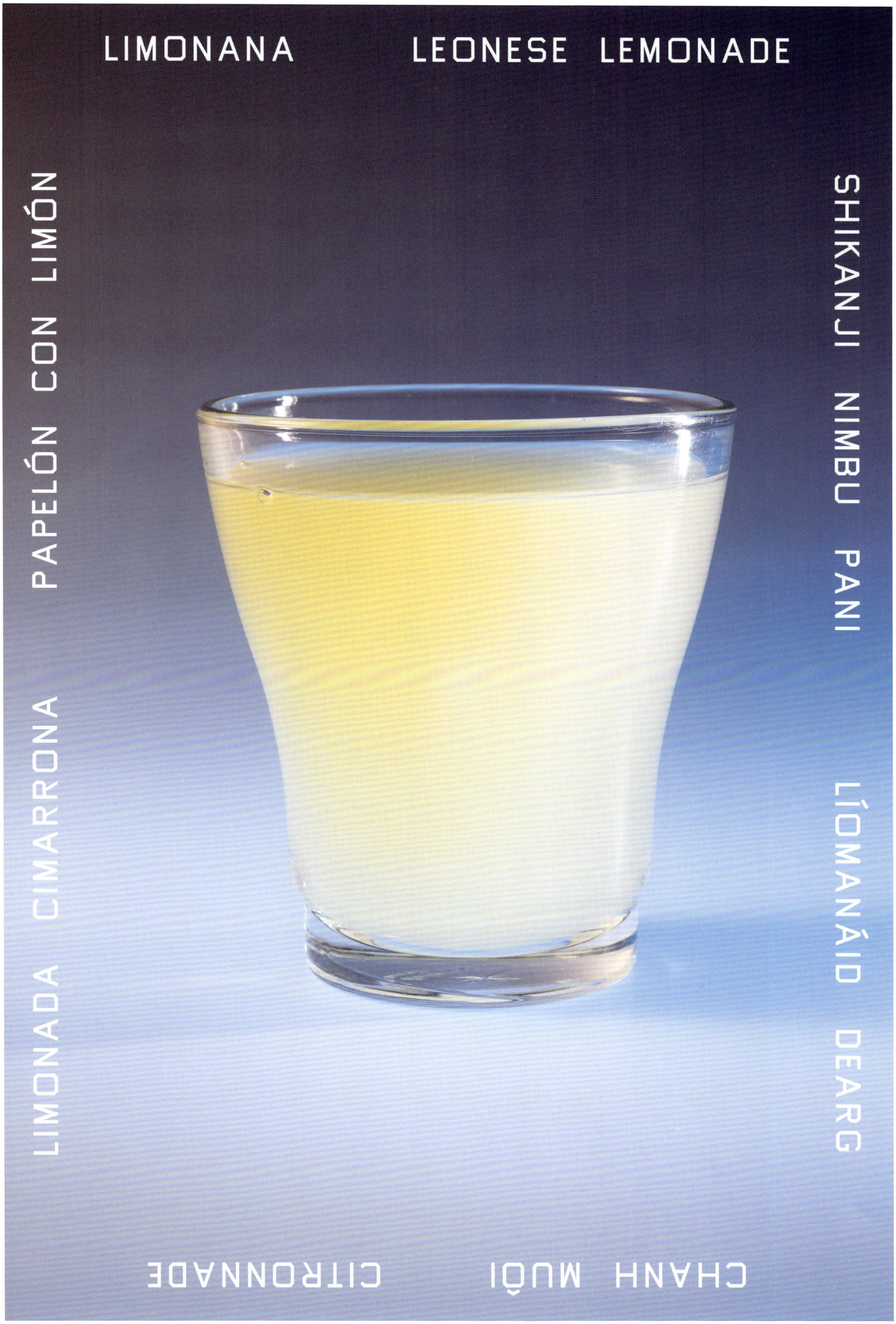

LIMONANA

LEONESE LEMONADE

SHIKANJI NIMBU PANI

LÍOMANÁID DEARG

CHANH MUỐI

CITRONNADE

LIMONADA CIMARRONA

PAPELÓN CON LIMÓN

THE AVERAGE

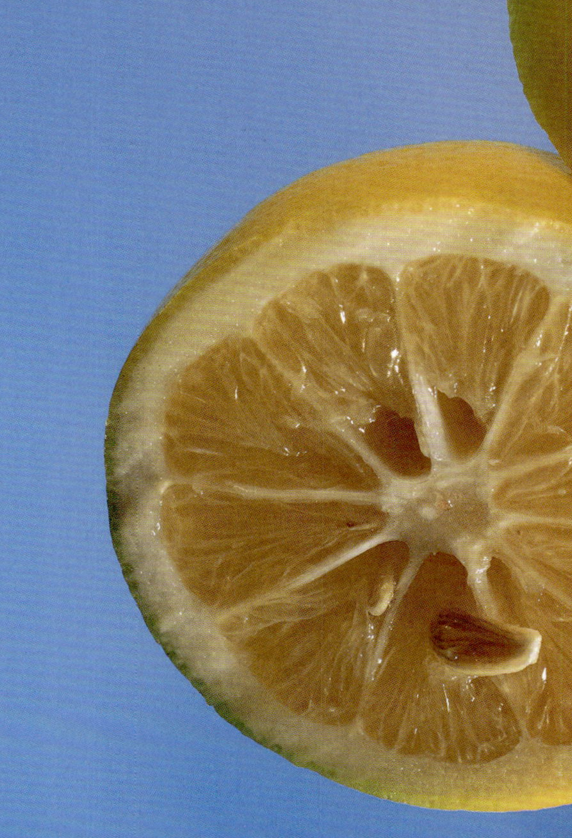

LEMON CONTAINS EIGHT

PIPS

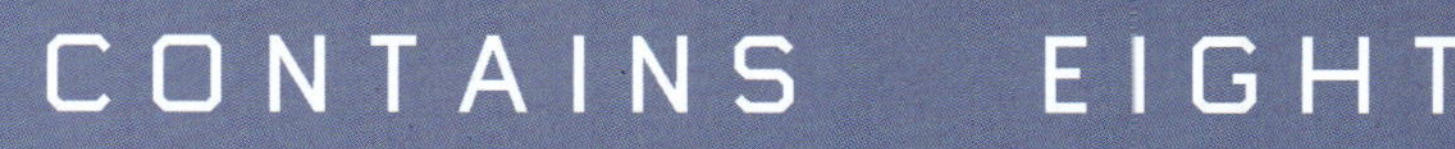

THE AVERAGE LEMON CONTAINS EIGHT SEEDS

Lemon almond cake

- 1¼ sticks/10 tablespoons unsalted butter, softened, plus more for the pan
- Zest and juice of 4 lemons
- 1 cup superfine sugar
- 5 egg yolks plus 3 egg whites
- 3 cups ground almonds
- ¾ cup self-raising flour
- 2 teaspoons baking powder

Preheat the oven to 350°.
Butter and line a standard-sized loaf pan.

In large saucepan, combine lemon zest, lemon juice, sugar, and egg yolks. Cook gently, stirring, over very low heat until thick. Remove from heat, stir in butter, pass through sieve and cool.

Add ground almonds and flour to lemon mixture.

Beat egg whites to soft peaks. Fold in baking powder, and combine with lemon almond mixture.

Pour into the prepared tin and bake 50 minutes.
Leave to cool in tin.

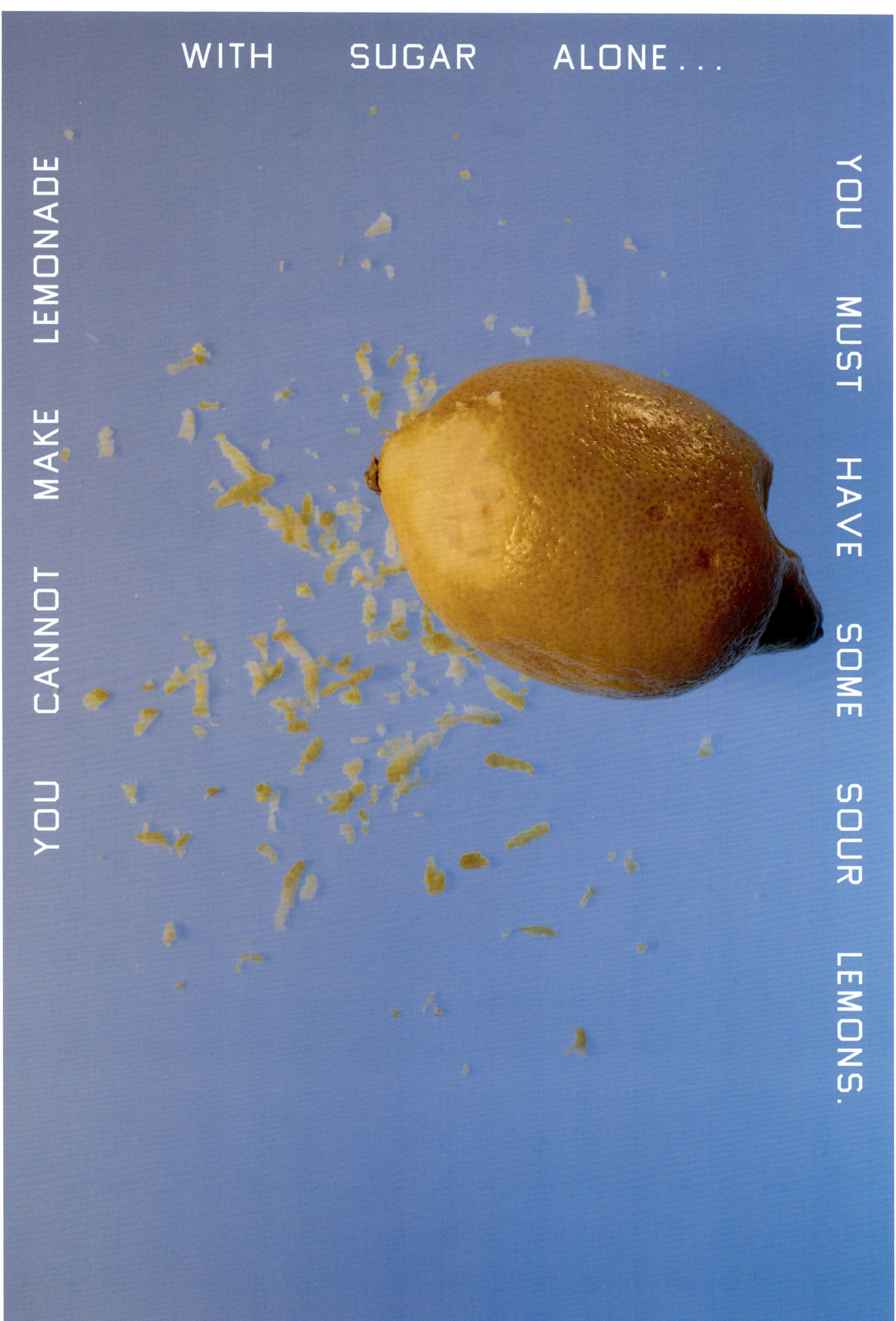
YOU CANNOT MAKE LEMONADE
WITH SUGAR ALONE...
YOU MUST HAVE SOME SOUR LEMONS.

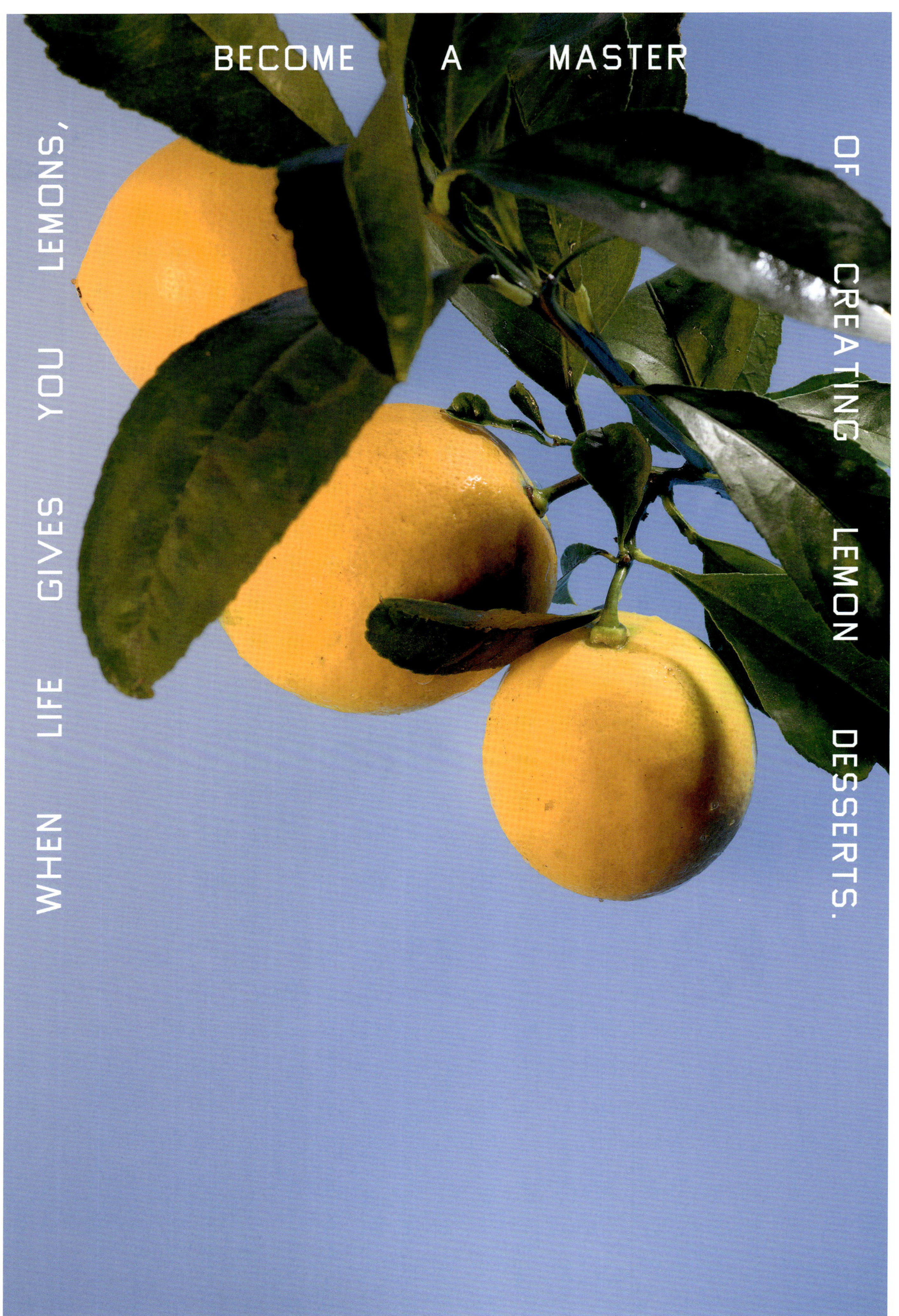
BECOME A MASTER
WHEN LIFE GIVES YOU LEMONS,
OF CREATING LEMON DESSERTS.

Lemon almond polenta cake

- 1 pound/4 sticks unsalted butter, softened, plus more for the pan
- All-purpose flour for the pan
- 2¼ cups superfine sugar
- 4½ cups ground almonds
- 2 teaspoons vanilla extract
- 6 eggs
- Zest of 4 lemons, plus juice of 1 lemon
- 1¼ cups polenta
- 1½ teaspoons baking powder
- ¼ teaspoon sea salt

Preheat oven to 325°.
Butter and flour 12-inch round cake tin.

Beat the butter and sugar together until pale and light. Stir in ground almonds and vanilla. Beat in eggs one at a time. Fold in the lemon zest and juice, polenta, baking powder and salt.

Spoon batter into prepared tin. Bake in the preheated oven for 45–50 minutes or until set and deep brown on top.

Lemon almond ricotta cake

- 2 sticks/1 cup unsalted butter, softened, plus more for pan
- 2¼ cups blanched almonds, finely ground
- ½ cup all-purpose flour
- 7 lemons, zested, and juice of 3
- 1 cup plus 2 tablespoons superfine sugar
- 6 eggs, separated
- 1¼ cups fresh ricotta

Preheat oven to 300°.
Butter and line 9-inch round cake tin.

Combine almonds with the flour and lemon zest.

Beat butter and sugar together until pale and light. Add egg yolks one by one, then incorporate almond mixture.

Beat ricotta lightly with fork, and add lemon juice.

In separate bowl, beat egg whites until they form soft peaks. Fold egg whites into almond mixture, then gently stir in the ricotta.

Spoon mixture into prepared tin. Bake for 35–40 minutes; test for doneness by inserting skewer, which should come out clean.

Remove from tin while still warm.

Lemon basil risotto

- 4 cups chicken stock
- 1 stick unsalted butter
- 1 red onion, finely chopped
- 1 tender celery stalk with leaves, separated and finely chopped
- 1 clove garlic, finely chopped
- 1½ cups carnaroli rice
- ⅔ cup dry vermouth
- 6 tablespoons roughly chopped fresh basil
- Zest and juice of 4 large lemons
- 4 ounces Parmesan, freshly grated
- 5 tablespoons mascarpone

Heat chicken stock. Melt half the butter in thick-bottomed saucepan over medium heat. Gently fry onion and celery stalk until soft. Add garlic and celery leaves, stir to combine, then add rice.

Stir rice to coat, then add vermouth. Allow to bubble and reduce, then add hot stock ladle by ladle over gentle heat. Stir constantly and allow each ladleful to be absorbed before adding another.

When rice is al dente, after approximately 20 minutes, stir in most of the basil, lemon juice and zest, half the Parmesan, and the mascarpone. Texture should be creamy. Serve with a few basil leaves and the remaining Parmesan.

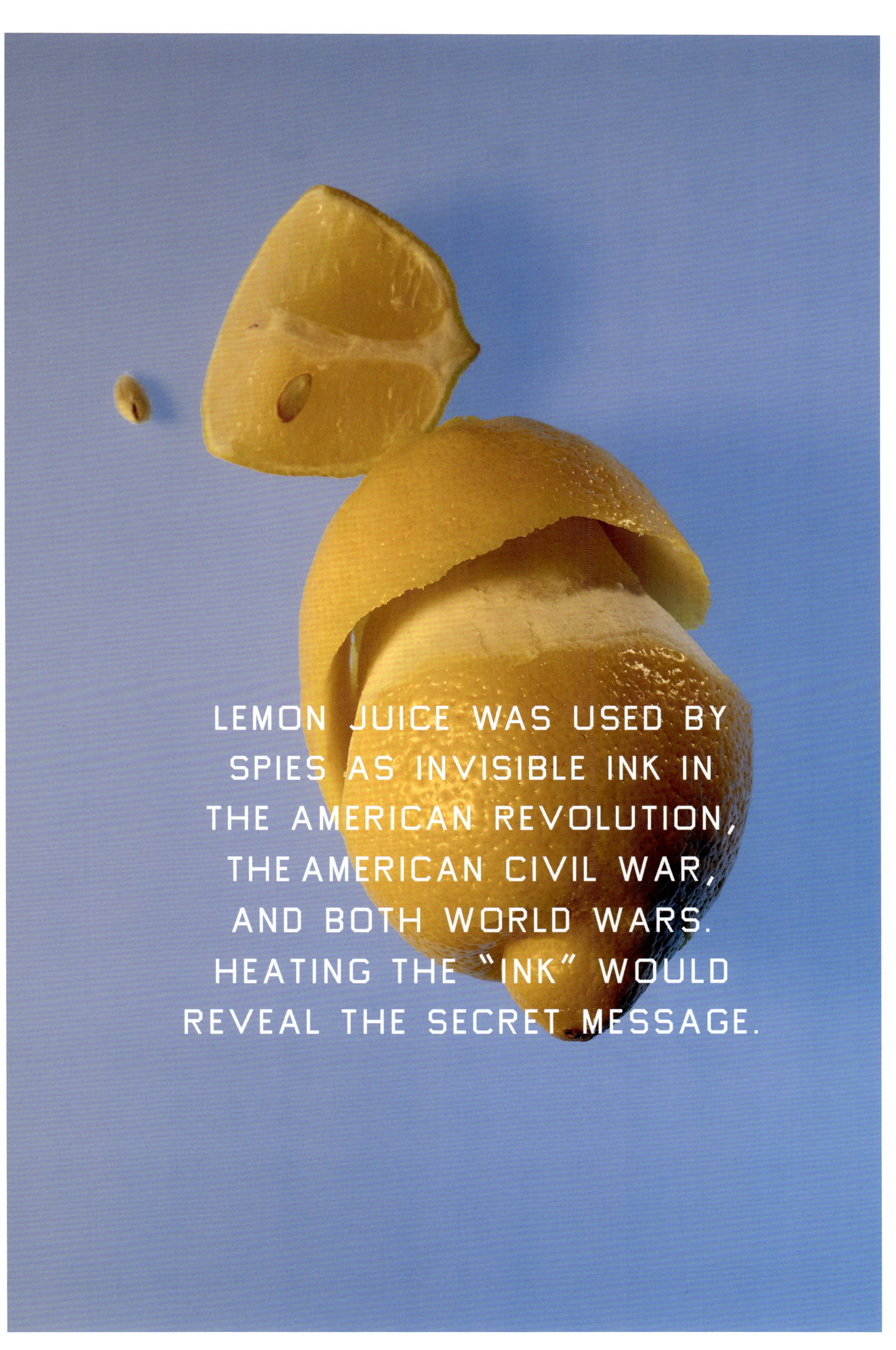
LEMON JUICE WAS USED BY
SPIES AS INVISIBLE INK IN
THE AMERICAN REVOLUTION,
THE AMERICAN CIVIL WAR,
AND BOTH WORLD WARS.
HEATING THE "INK" WOULD
REVEAL THE SECRET MESSAGE.

Lemon fennel seed biscuits

- 3 tablespoons fennel seeds
- 1¾ pounds/7 sticks butter
- Zest of 8 lemons
- 240g sugar
- 1½ teaspoons salt
- 1¾ cup almonds
- 8 cups all-purpose flour
- Turbinado sugar, for rolling

Toast and roughly grind fennel seeds.

In mixer, beat butter, fennel, lemon zest, sugar, and salt until soft and creamy.

Grind almonds with flour until fine.

Incorporate dry ingredients into butter mixture until just combined. Roll dough into logs 2 inches in diameter. Store in freezer until ready to bake.

To bake, preheat oven to 325°. Allow logs to defrost slightly, then roll edges in turbinado sugar and slice into rounds. Bake 12–15 minutes until lightly golden.

Lemon granita

- ⅓ cup superfine sugar
- Finely grated zest of 1 lemon
- 1 cup lemon juice

Bring water and sugar to boil in heavy-bottomed saucepan; cook until reduced by almost half. Remove from heat and, when cool, add lemon juice and zest.

Pour into shallow container, and put in freezer. Allow the liquid to partially freeze, about 20–30 minutes. Mash with fork to break up ice crystals, then return to freezer for 20 more minutes. Repeat this process, mashing up the frozen liquid, then freezing, until granita is hard, dry, and crystalline, approximately 2½ hours.

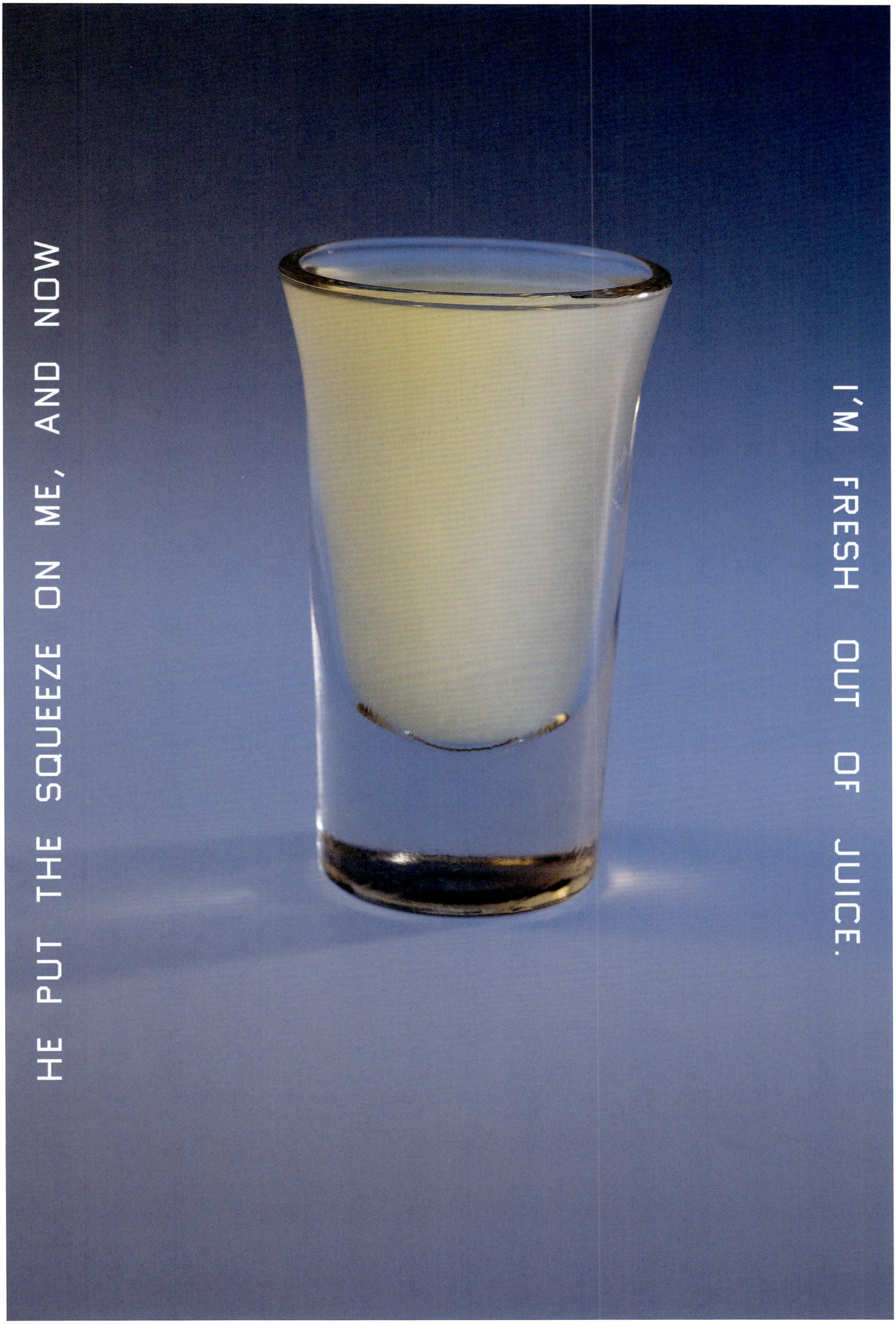

HE PUT THE SQUEEZE ON ME, AND NOW

I'M FRESH OUT OF JUICE.

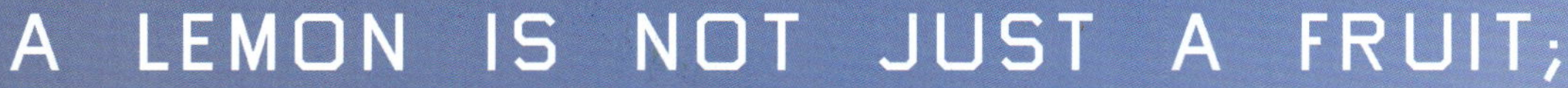

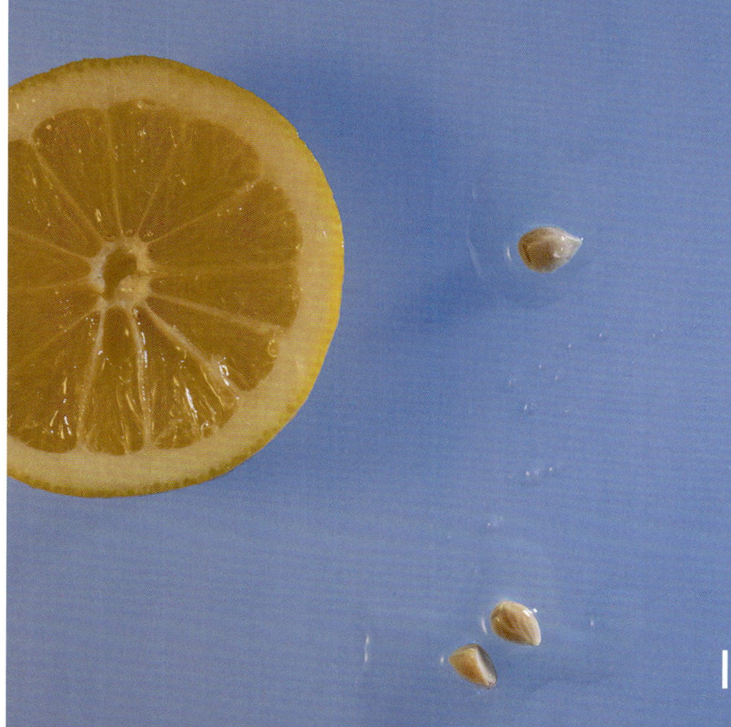

IT IS A MOOD.

Lemon ice cream

- 1 cup superfine sugar
- Zest and juice of 3 lemons
- 2 cups heavy cream
- ½ teaspoon sea salt

Combine sugar with lemon zest and juice. Slowly add the cream and ½ tsp salt, mixing carefully. It will immediately thicken.

Churn in ice-cream machine until frozen.

Lemon mascarpone tart

Pastry:
- 3 cups all-purpose flour
- 2 sticks/1 cup cold unsalted butter, cut into cubes
- ¾ cup plus 2 tablespoons confectioners' sugar, sifted
- 3 egg yolks

Filling:
- 6 whole eggs, plus 6 egg yolks
- 1¾ cups superfine sugar
- 1¼ cups mascarpone
- Zest and juice of 6 lemons
- 2 tablespoons confectioners' sugar

Make pastry: pulse flour, salt and butter in food processor until mixture resembles coarse breadcrumbs. Add confectioners' sugar followed by the egg yolks and pulse until combined. Wrap pastry and chill in fridge for at least an hour.

Preheat oven to 325°. Coarsely grate pastry into a 12-inch loose-bottomed fluted tart pan, then press evenly onto sides and base. Chill 15 minutes. Line pastry shell with parchment paper and fill with raw rice or baking beans. Bake blind for 20 minutes or until very light brown. Remove from oven, remove paper and rice, and allow to cool. Reduce oven to 300°.

To make filling, beat eggs and yolks with sugar. Add mascarpone, stir to combine, then add lemon juice and zest.

Pour into tart shell and bake for an hour. Cool, sprinkle with confectioners' sugar, and serve.

HOPE WILL NEVER DIE.

AS LONG AS THE LEMON TREE GROWS

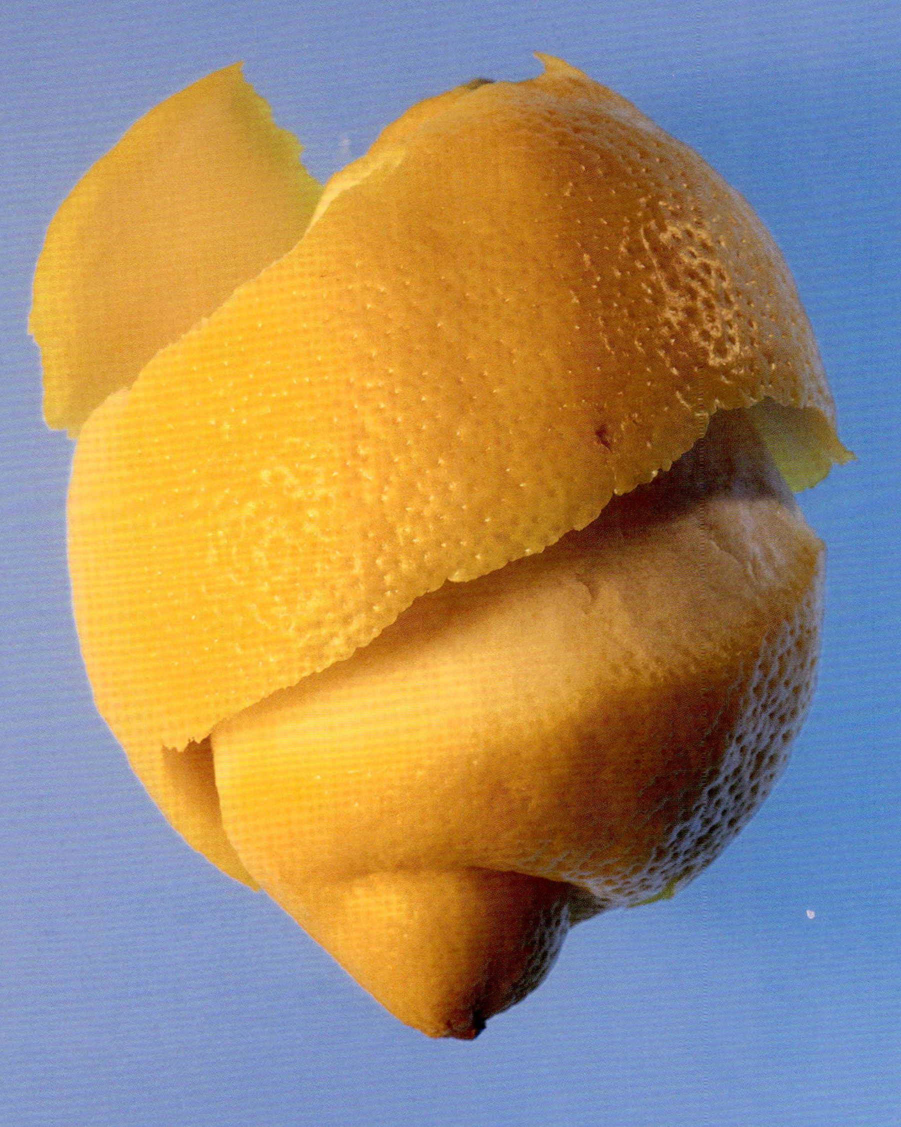

ZOULFA KATOUH

Lemon, ricotta, and pine nut cake

- Unsalted butter for pan
- 1⅔ cups white breadcrumbs
- 2½ cups ricotta
- 1 cup superfine sugar
- 4 eggs plus 2 egg yolks
- 1 cup crème fraiche
- Zest and juice of 3 lemons
- 2 cups mascarpone
- ⅓ cup pine nuts

Preheat the oven to 300°. Butter sides and bottom of 10-inch springform cake tin. Shake breadcrumbs around tin to coat sides evenly; pour out any excess.

Whisk ricotta with sugar until smooth. Add eggs and egg yolks one at a time and continue beating. Add crème fraiche. Finally, fold in the lemon mixture and mascarpone.

Pour batter into tin and scatter pine nuts on top. Bake 45 minutes until just set but wobbly.

Cool and turn out.

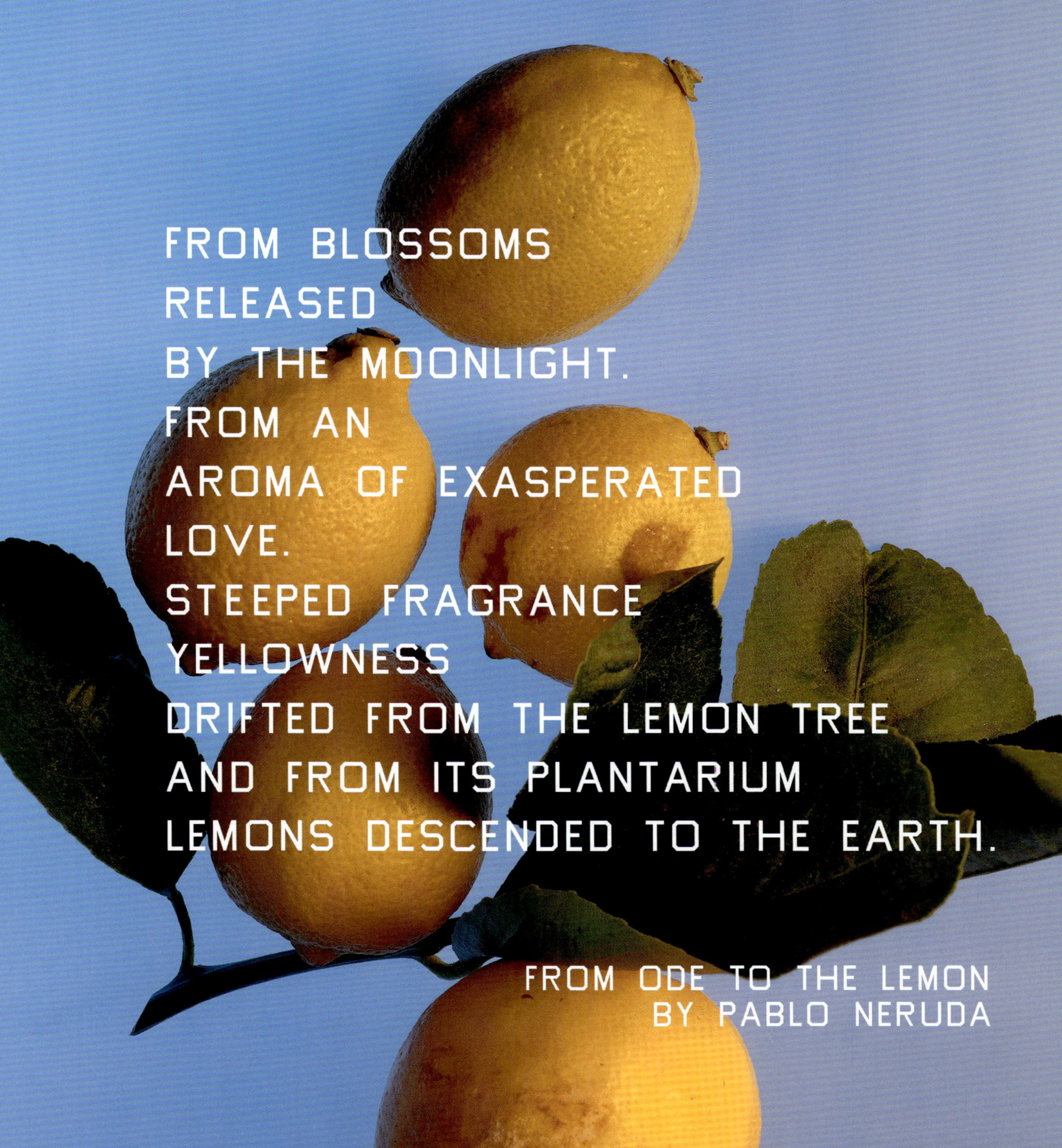
FROM BLOSSOMS
RELEASED
BY THE MOONLIGHT.
FROM AN
AROMA OF EXASPERATED
LOVE.
STEEPED FRAGRANCE
YELLOWNESS
DRIFTED FROM THE LEMON TREE
AND FROM ITS PLANTARIUM
LEMONS DESCENDED TO THE EARTH.
FROM ODE TO THE LEMON
BY PABLO NERUDA

Lemon ricotta ice cream

- 7¼ cups heavy cream
- 2 cups whole milk
- 20 egg yolks
- 1¾ cups superfine sugar
- 2 cups ricotta, roughly crumbled
- Zest and juice of 7 lemons

In heavy saucepan, heat cream and milk until just below boiling point. Remove from the heat. Whisk the egg yolks and sugar until light and fluffy, about 10 minutes. Mix a little warm cream into eggs, then transfer whole lot, including remaining cream, back to saucepan.

Cook over very low flame, stirring constantly to prevent curdling. When mixture is thick, remove from heat and pass through fine sieve. Cool overnight.

Add lemon zest and juice and ricotta to cream mixture; stir to combine. Churn in ice-cream machine until frozen.

Lemon semifreddo

- 4 eggs, separated
- 1 cup superfine sugar
- Zest and juice of 4 lemons
- 1 cup heavy cream
- 1 teaspoon sea salt

Beat egg yolks with sugar until light, at least 8 minutes. Place mixture in bowl over large saucepan of simmering water (bowl should not touch water). Whisk continuously until mixture comes to boil.

Cool, then add lemon mixture.
Lightly beat cream and fold in.

Beat egg whites with 1 teaspoon salt until stiff; fold into lemon and egg yolk mixture.

Line tin with parchment, pour in mixture and freeze until firm.

Lemon sorbet

- 2 whole lemons, quartered, plus 4 cups fresh lemon juice
- 5¼ cups superfine sugar
- 2½ ripe bananas, peeled

Place lemons, sugar, and bananas in food processor (it is easier to do this in two batches). Blend until mixture is coarse with very small bits of lemon peel still visible.

Put mixture in large bowl and stir in lemon juice.
Churn in ice-cream machine until frozen.

A GRAPEFRUIT IS

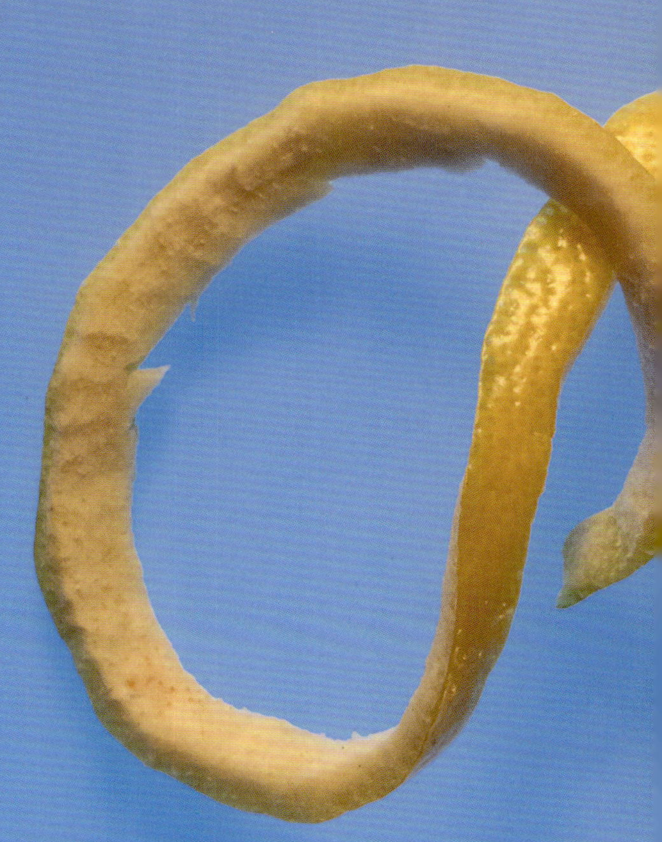

OSCAR WILDE

J U S T A L E M O N

T H A T S A W A N O P P O R T U N I T Y

A N D T O O K A D V A N T A G E O F I T

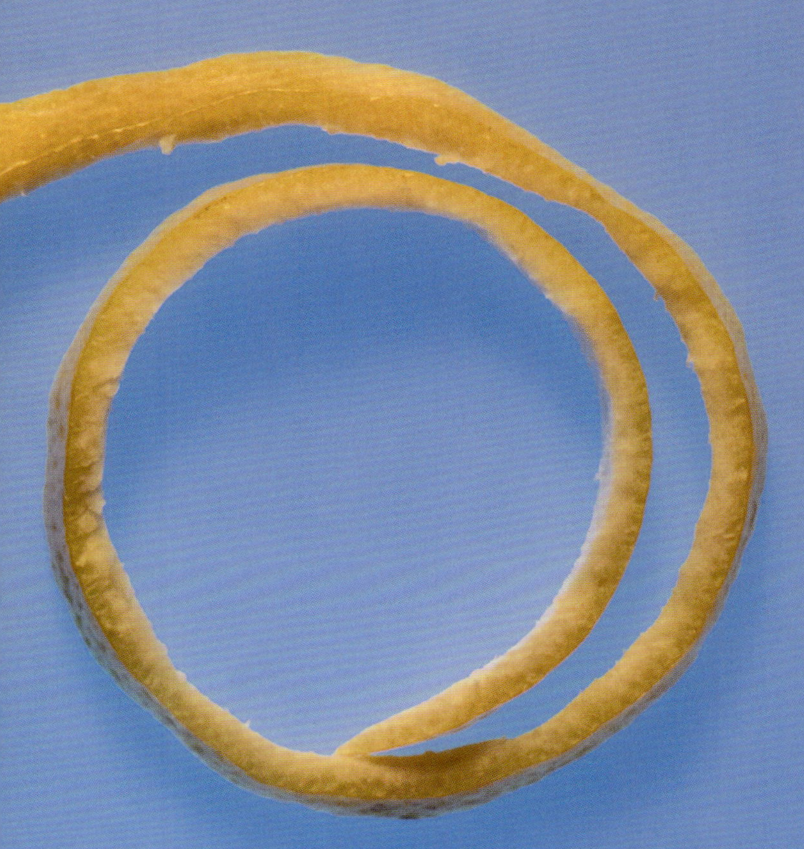

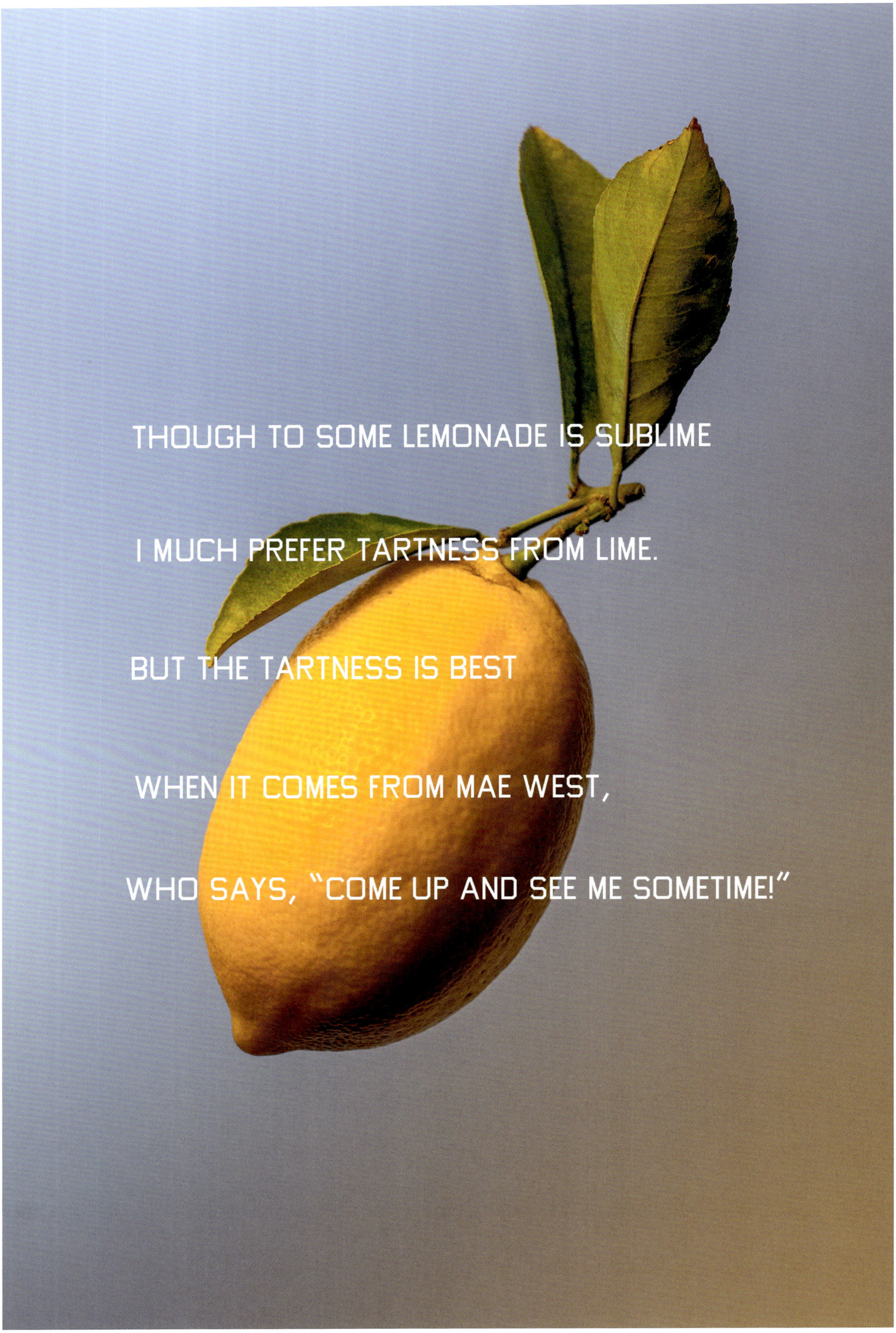

THOUGH TO SOME LEMONADE IS SUBLIME

I MUCH PREFER TARTNESS FROM LIME.

BUT THE TARTNESS IS BEST

WHEN IT COMES FROM MAE WEST,

WHO SAYS, "COME UP AND SEE ME SOMETIME!"

Lemon tart

- 1 recipe pastry dough (see Lemon mascarpone tart, page 42), well chilled
- Finely grated zest and juice of 7 lemons
- 1¾ cups granulated sugar
- 6 whole eggs
- 9 egg yolks
- 2 sticks plus 5 tablespoons unsalted butter, softened

Preheat oven to 325°. Coarsely grate pastry into a 12-inch loose-bottomed fluted tart pan, then press evenly onto sides and base. Chill 15 minutes. Line pastry shell with parchment paper and fill with raw rice or baking beans. Bake blind for 20 minutes or until very light brown. Remove from oven, remove paper and rice, and bake for a further 10 minutes or until golden brown. Leave to cool.

Meanwhile, make filling. Put all remaining ingredients, except butter, in a large saucepan over very low heat; whisk until the eggs have broken up and the sugar has dissolved.

Add half the butter and continue to whisk. As eggs start to cook, mixture will thicken enough to coat back of spoon. Add remaining butter and continue whisking until the mixture is very thick. Whisk throughout cooking process to prevent curdling.

Remove pan from heat, continuing to whisk. Meanwhile, preheat oven grill to full heat. Spoon lemon filling into the pastry shell and leave to settle. When grill is very hot, grill tart until the top is mottled brown, about 3–5 minutes. Cool before serving.

Limoncello

- 16 lemons, washed and dried
- 1 liter vodka
- 1½ cups sugar

Using peeler, remove lemon peel, avoiding pith. Place peels in large jar or airtight container.

Add vodka to jar with peels. Seal and leave at room temperature, out of direct sunlight, at least 5 days and up to 1 month.

Sieve infused vodka into large container, discarding lemon peels. Pour infused vodka back into jar, seal, and refrigerate.

To make syrup, combine sugar with 1 cup water in medium saucepan. Bring to simmer, stirring occasionally, until sugar is dissolved. Cool completely.

When syrup is cooled, stir into infused vodka. Refrigerate and serve very cold in shot glasses.

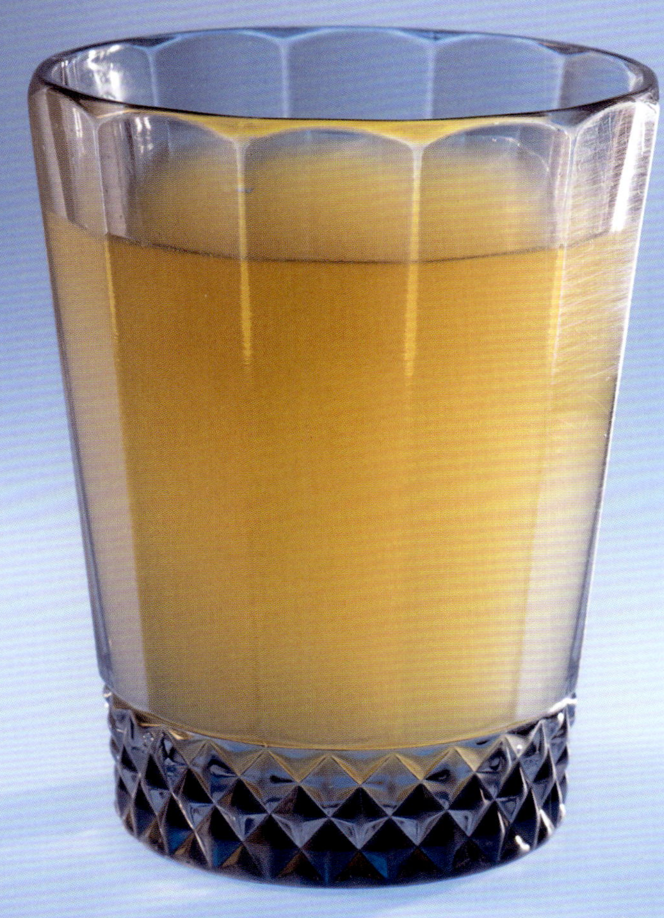
ICONIC ANIONIC
VITAMIN C BIONIC

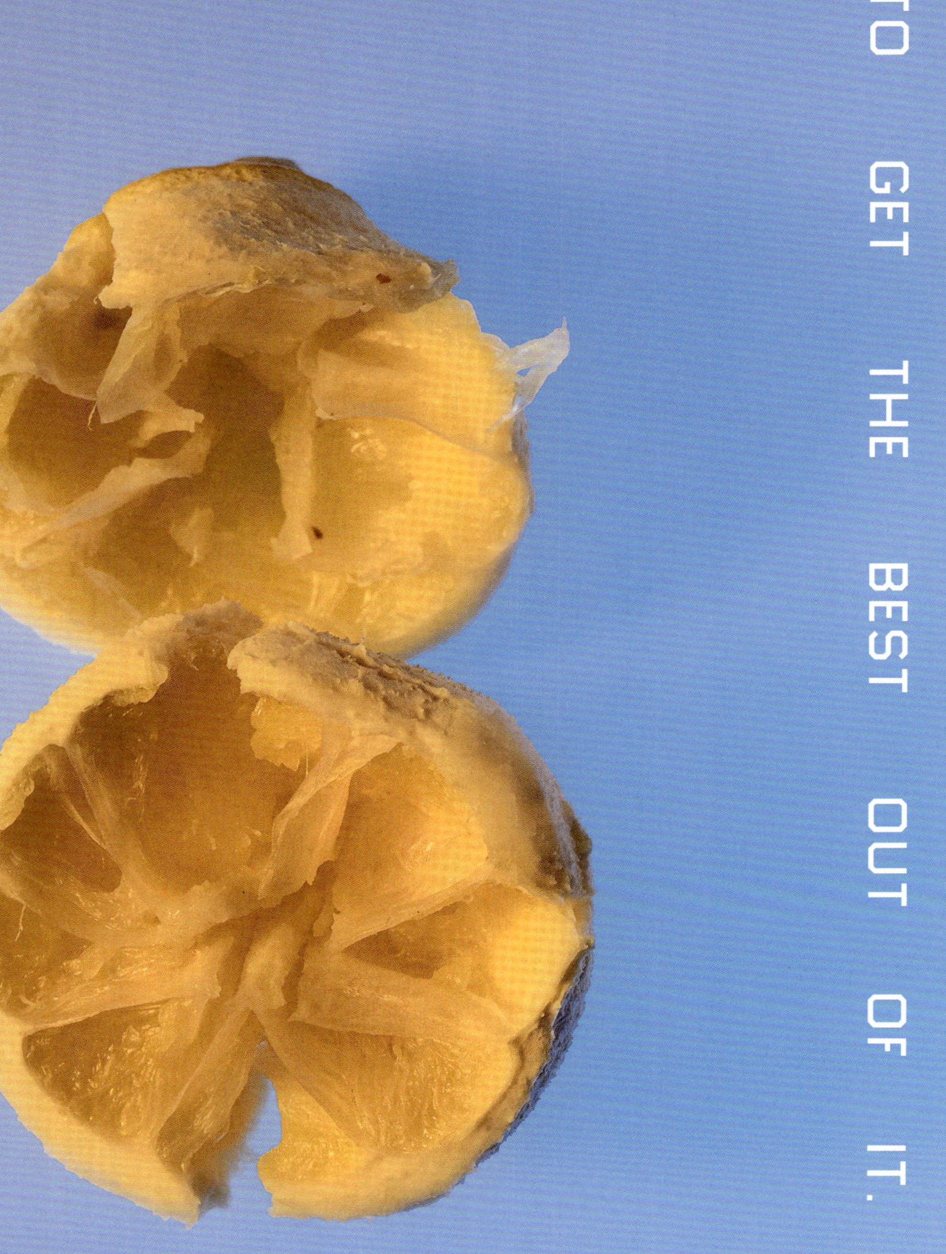
A LEMON IS A BEAUTIFUL FRUIT,
BUT YOU HAVE TO SQUEEZE IT
TO GET THE BEST OUT OF IT.

Marinated artichokes with lemon and thyme

- 12 small globe artichokes, stalks attached
- Sea salt
- 1 small bunch marjoram
- 1 small bunch oregano
- 1 small bunch summer savory
- 1 small bunch thyme
- Cloves from 2 heads garlic, peeled and thickly sliced
- Freshly ground black pepper
- Juice of 4 lemons
- About 4 cups extra virgin olive oil
- Lemon wedges for serving

Prepare artichokes. Cut stalks, leaving about 2 inches, then peel, leaving pale tender center. Break off tough outer leaves, starting at the base, to expose pale inner heart. Trim tough or sharp tops from artichokes. Cut artichokes in half from tip to stalk, and remove any prickly choke using teaspoon.

Blanch in boiling salted water about 5 minutes, or until a leaf pulls out easily. Drain and dry well.

In large bowl, layer artichokes, the herbs, garlic, and salt and pepper. Add lemon juice and extra virgin olive oil (approx. 1 liter) to cover. Marinate artichokes a minimum of 3 hours, up to 4–5 days.

Serve with a little of the oil and fresh lemon wedges.

Marinated grilled lamb with lemon and rosemary

- 1 (5-pound) leg of spring lamb, boned and butterflied
- 5 cloves garlic, peeled and crushed
- 2 tablespoons chopped rosemary leaves
- Coarsely ground black pepper
- Juice of 2 lemons
- Extra virgin olive oil
- Sea salt
- Lemon wedges for serving

Place meat in shallow dish; rub crushed garlic, rosemary, and coarse black pepper over cut side, then pour over lemon juice and a little olive oil.

Turn meat over a couple of times to make sure it is coated, then cover and leave to marinate in refrigerator overnight, or for at least 4 hours, turning meat occasionally.

Prepare charcoal fire in barbecue or heat large griddle pan until very hot. Remove meat from the marinade and pat dry. Season with the salt. Carefully place meat on grill and brown on both sides.

Lower heat and continue to grill until meat reaches the desired degree of pinkness, turning as needed. Allow at least 8 minutes per side. Rest lamb several minutes. Serve with lemon wedges.

Marjoram lemon salmoriglio

- ¼ cup marjoram leaves
- Juice of 1 lemon
- Freshly ground black pepper

With a pestle and mortar, pound herb leaves with salt until completely crushed. Add lemon juice. Slowly incorporate olive oil to cover. Add a little pepper.

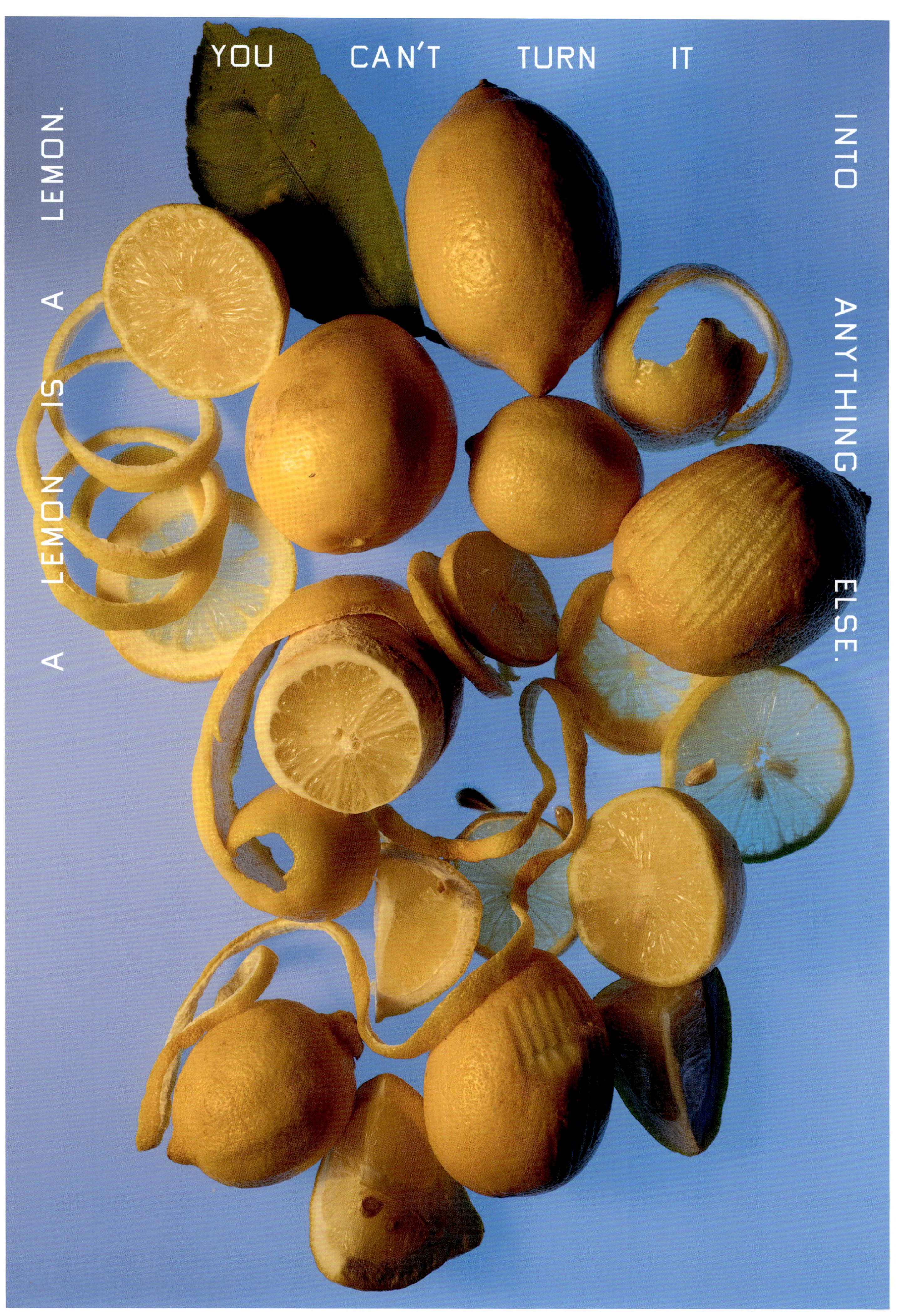
A LEMON IS A LEMON.
YOU CAN'T TURN IT
INTO ANYTHING ELSE.

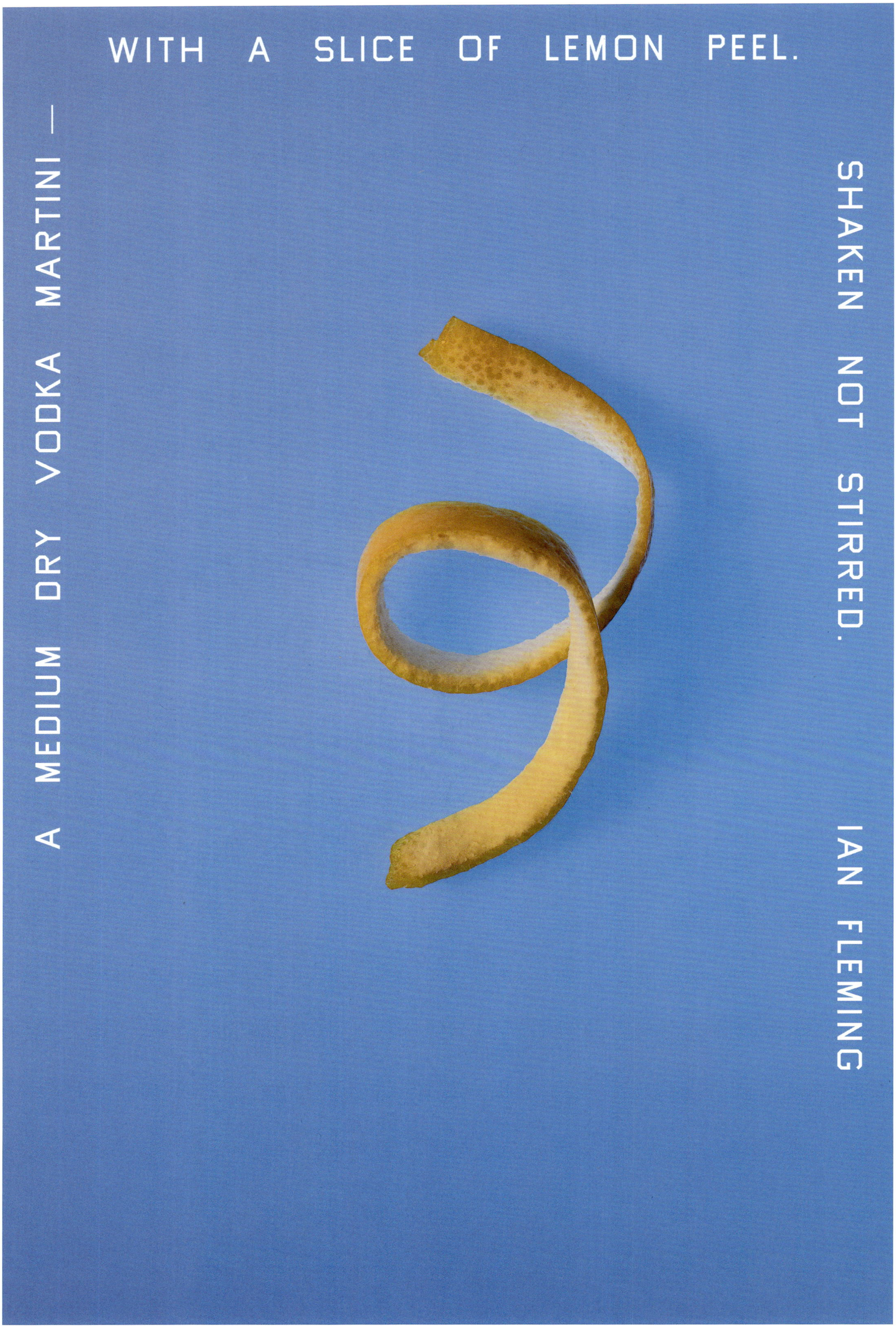

A MEDIUM DRY VODKA MARTINI — WITH A SLICE OF LEMON PEEL. SHAKEN NOT STIRRED.

IAN FLEMING

Martini

- ½ ounce dry vermouth
- 2½ ounces vodka or gin, as preferred
- Peel of 1 lemon

Fill a cocktail mixing glass with ice.

Add vermouth and stir. Strain the vermouth away.

Add gin or vodka to the mixing glass and stir until very cold.

Pour the mixture into a chilled Martini glass using a double strainer.

To add a lemon twist cut a piece of lemon peel, squeeze the back of the peel over the top of the cocktail to release the oils, and add to the glass to serve.

Panna cotta with lemon peel and grappa

- 5 cups heavy cream
- 2 vanilla pods
- Peel of 2 lemons, thinly sliced
- 3 leaves gelatin
- ⅔ cup cold whole milk
- 1¼ cups confectioners' sugar
- ½ cup grappa, plus more for serving

Pour 4 cups cream into a pan with vanilla pods and lemon rind. Bring to boil, then simmer until reduced by one-third. Remove cooked lemon rind and keep to one side. Remove vanilla pods and scrape their softened insides back into the cream.

Soak gelatin in milk about 15 minutes or until soft. Remove gelatin, bring milk to boil, then return gelatin to the milk and stir until dissolved. Pour gelatin mixture through sieve into into hot cream through a sieve. Stir, then allow to sit off heat.

Lightly whip remaining cream with the icing sugar. Fold into cooked cream, then add grappa.

Place a piece of cooked lemon rind in each of six small 1-cup moulds. Pour in the cream mixture and set in fridge for at least 2 hours.

Turn out onto dessert plates and serve with grappa poured over the top.

THE BRITISH NAVY GAVE ITS SAILORS LEMON JUICE OR LIMES TO WARD OFF SCURVY EARNING THEM THE NICKNAME "LIMEY" AMONG SKEPTICAL AMERICAN SAILORS.

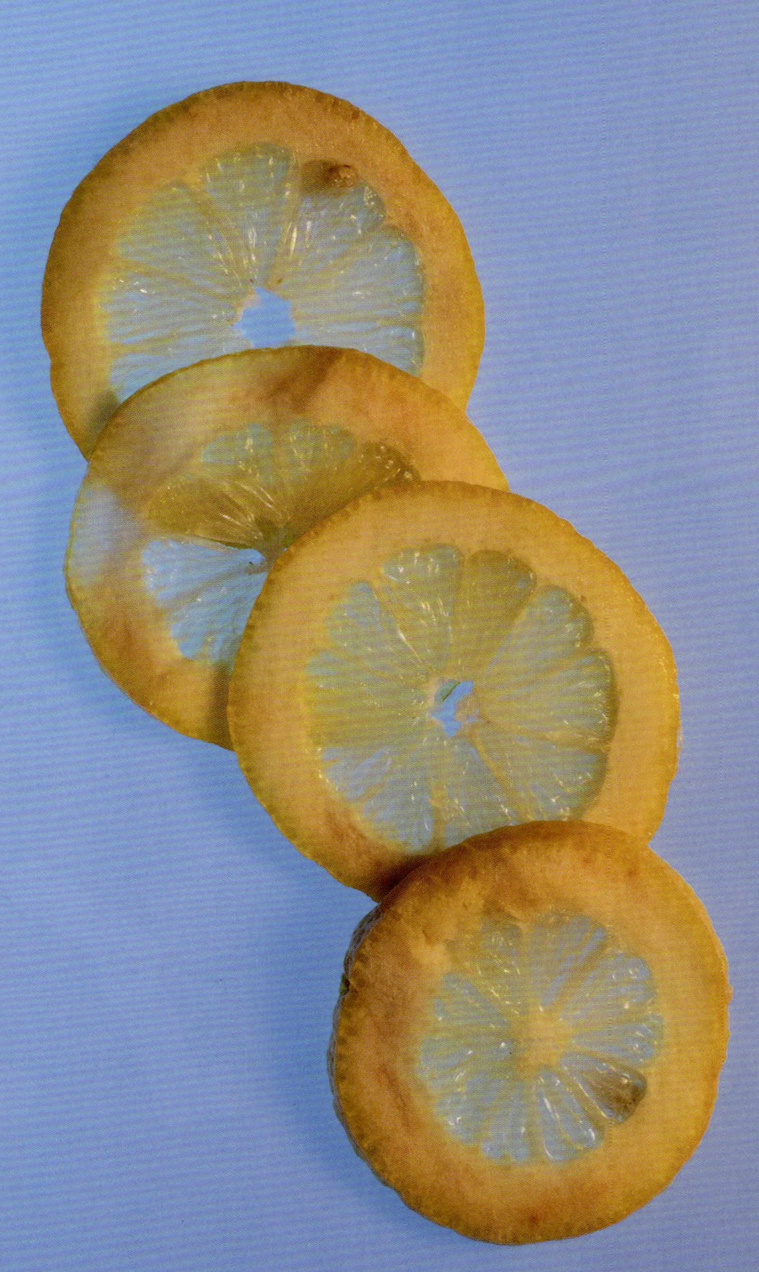

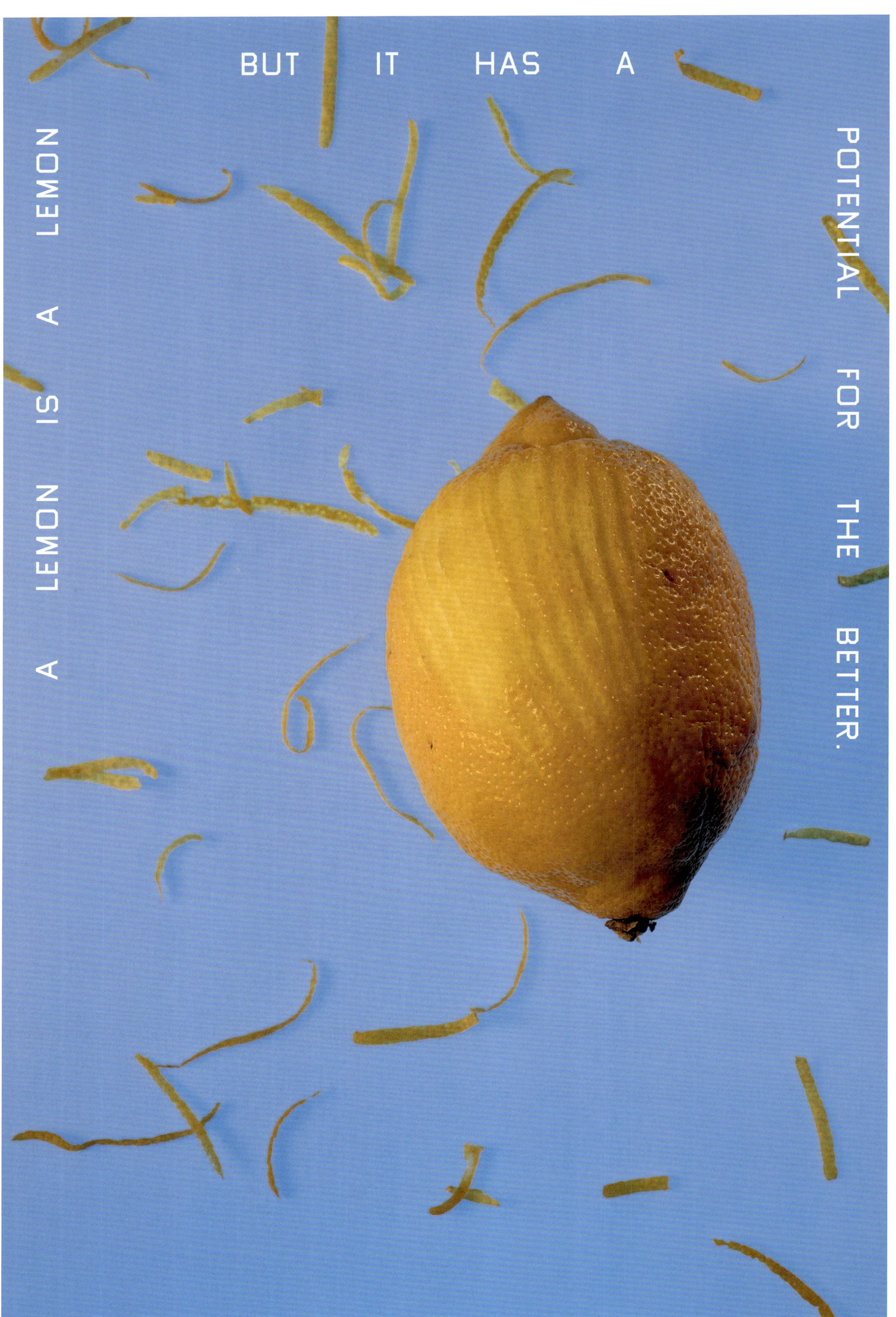
A LEMON IS A LEMON
BUT IT HAS A
POTENTIAL FOR THE BETTER.

Pea, ricotta, and lemon zest risotto

- 6⅓ cups chicken stock
- 1½ teaspoons sea salt, plus more to taste
- 6½ pounds fresh young peas
- 2 tablespoons chopped mint leaves
- 2 cloves garlic, chopped, plus 1 clove left whole
- 1 stick plus 6 tablespoons unsalted butter
- 1 pound spring onions or scallions, roughly chopped
- 2 cups carnaroli rice
- Freshly ground black pepper
- 2 tablespoons torn fresh basil leaves
- ⅔ cup dry vermouth
- 1 cup ricotta, lightly beaten
- Finely grated zest of 2 lemons
- 2 ounces Parmesan, freshly grated

Heat chicken stock to simmer. Bring medium saucepan of water to boil, then add 1½ teaspoons salt, peas, half the mint and the whole garlic clove. Cook 3–4 minutes or until peas are al dente. Drain, reserving ⅔ cup of the water. Return peas, mint, and garlic clove to reserved water and put aside.

Melt 10 tablespoons butter in large thick-bottomed saucepan. Add onion and soften, then stir in chopped garlic. Add rice, salt, and pepper, stirring to coat each grain for about 2–3 minutes. Add a ladle of hot stock and stir, adding another when the rice has absorbed the first. Continue stirring and adding stock for 10 minutes or until the rice is not quite al dente.

Add half the peas, the cooked garlic, mint, and the cooking liquid. Puree the remainder of the peas, mint, and garlic with the liquid in the food processor, then stir into risotto.

Add basil, vermouth, about 2 tablespoons ricotta, and the remaining butter. Cook briefly to wilt basil and melt butter.

Test for doneness: the rice should be al dente. Serve with the remaining ricotta over each portion, sprinkled with lemon zest and Parmesan.

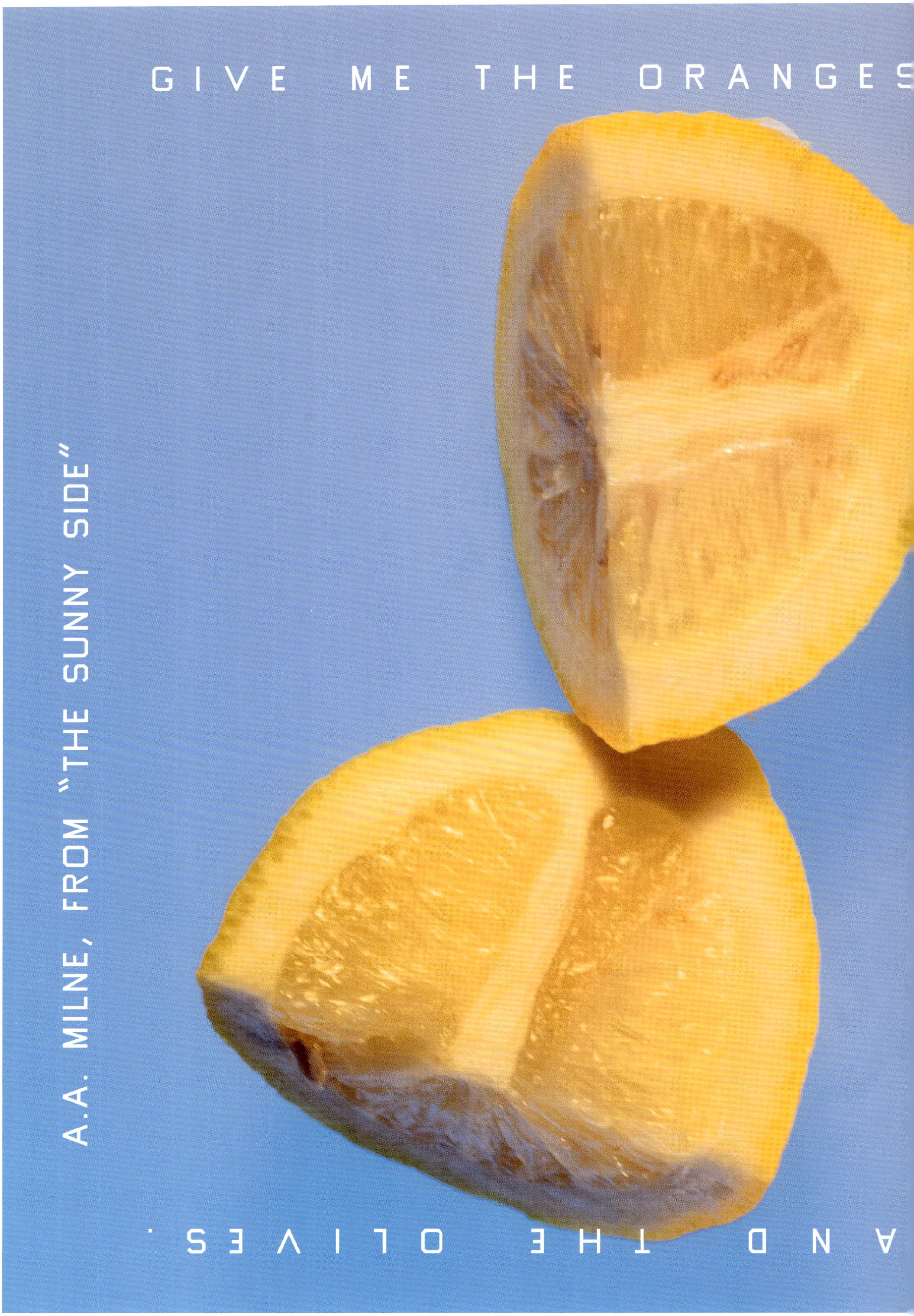

GIVE ME THE ORANGES AND THE OLIVES.

A.A. MILNE, FROM "THE SUNNY SIDE"

AND LEMONS, AND

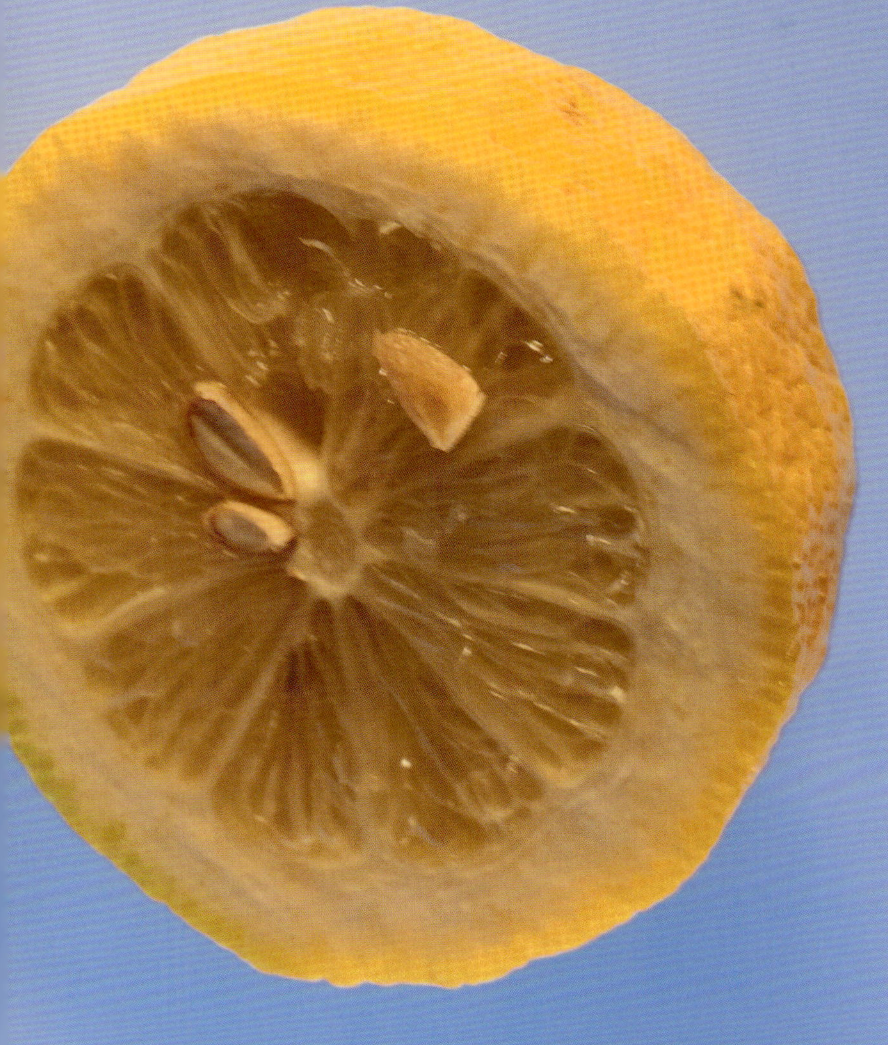

YOU CAN HAVE ALL

THE PALMS AND THE CACTUSES

Penne with zucchini and lemon zest

- 14 medium zucchini (yellow, green, or ridged varieties), trimmed
- 2 sticks/16 tablespoons unsalted butter
- Sea salt and freshly ground black pepper
- 2 garlic cloves, thinly sliced
- 12 ounces penne
- 1 bunch mint leaves
- Zest of 2 lemons
- 7 ounces Parmesan, freshly grated

Cut zucchini into ½-inch pieces. Heat olive oil with 7 tablespoons butter in large saucepan. Add zucchini and stir to coat. Season with sea salt and black pepper and add the garlic slices. Cook gently about 20 minutes, stirring from time to time until zucchini becomes a mushy puree consistency.

Meanwhile, bring saucepan of salted water to boil. Cook penne in boiling water until al dente, then drain and add to zucchini sauce. Add remaining butter and torn mint leaves. Mix thoroughly.

Transfer to the serving plates. Serve with lemon zest and freshly grated Parmesan

SEEDY

A CERTAIN PEEL

SOUR PATCH

PULP FICTION

ACID REIGN

WELL PRESERVED

PUCKER UP

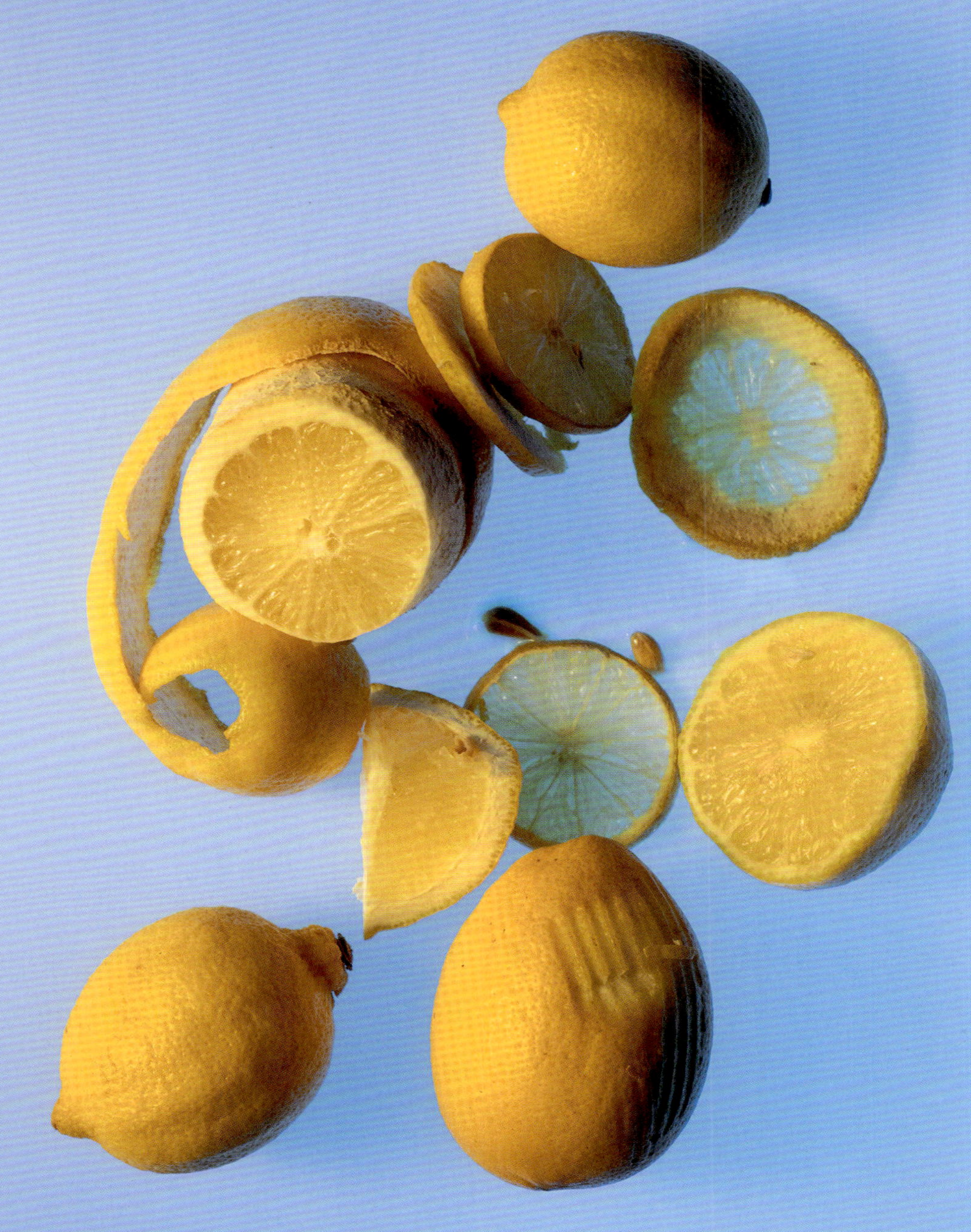

DRIZZLE

BUMPER CROP

FINELY GRATED

VITAMIN C

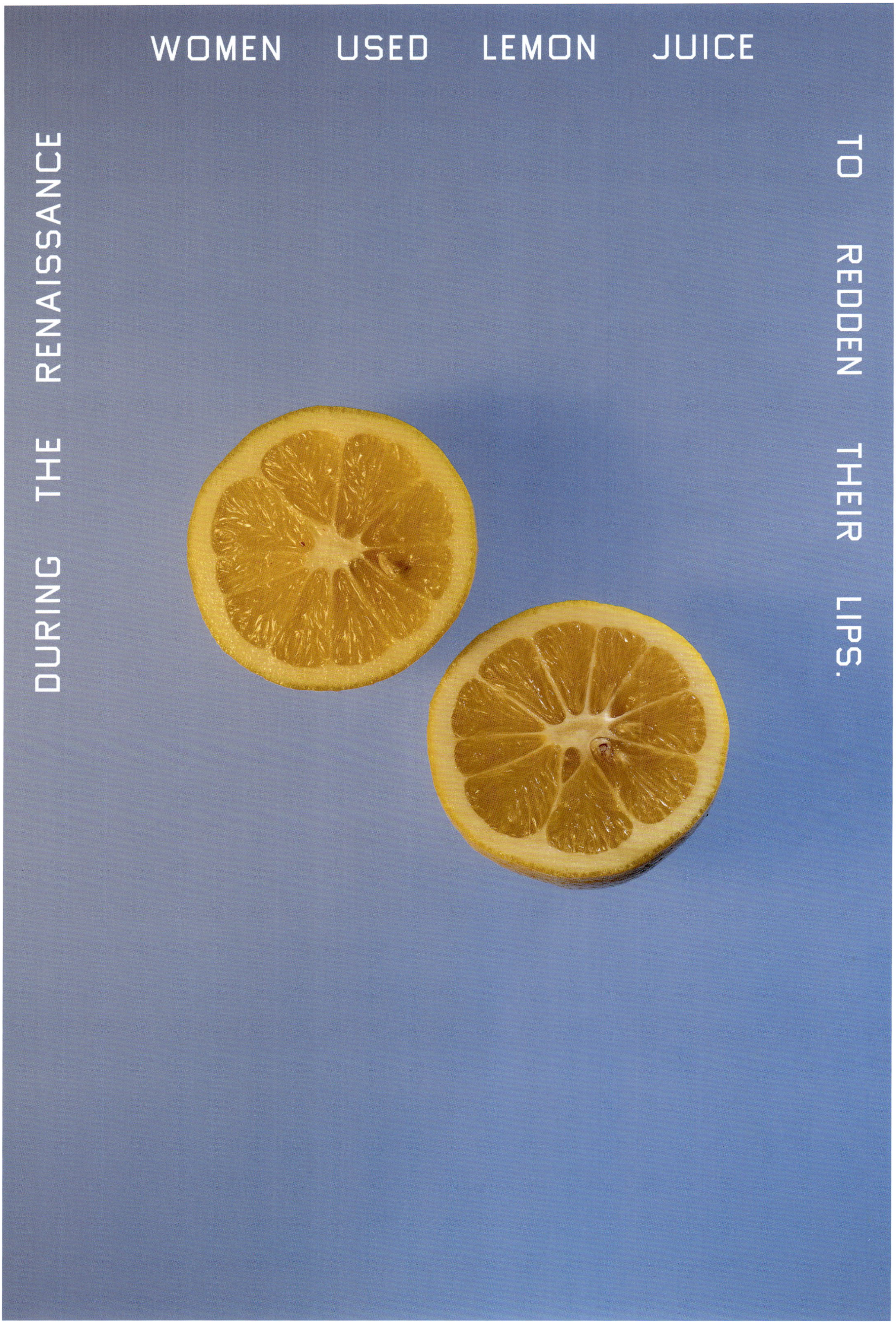

DURING THE RENAISSANCE WOMEN USED LEMON JUICE TO REDDEN THEIR LIPS.

Pici with lemon and pecorino

- Juice of 2 to 3 lemons
- 3½ cups fresh pecorino, coarsely grated
- ¼ cup extra virgin olive oil
- Sea salt
- 12 ounces pici or bucatini
- Leaves of 1 bunch fresh basil
- 2 ounces aged pecorino, finely grated
- Freshly ground black pepper

Cook pici in large pan of boiling salted water until al dente.

In saucepan over low heat, combine lemon juice and fresh pecorino, stirring until cheese melts into juice. Remove from heat. Gradually add ¼ cup olive oil slowly until it has combined, making a thick lumpy sauce. Set sauce aside somewhere warm.

Drain pasta, reserving a little cooking water. Return drained pici to pan and add 2 tablespoons hot cooking water. Add the sauce and basil leaves; toss until all pici strands are coated. Finally, stir in half the grated aged pecorino.

Serve sprinkled with remaining aged pecorino.

Pork cooked in milk with lemon peel

- 6¼ cups whole milk
- 1 (4- to 5-pound) boned loin of young organic pork, rind and most of the fat removed
- Sea salt and freshly ground black pepper
- Extra virgin olive oil
- 4 tablespoons unsalted butter
- 5 garlic cloves, halved
- 1 small handful sage leaves
- Peel of 2 lemons, pith removed

Generously season pork on all sides. Heat a splash of olive oil in a heavy-bottomed saucepan just large enough to hold the pork. Brown meat on all sides, then remove and discard excess fat.

In the same pan, melt butter. Add garlic and sage leaves; before garlic begins to color, return pork to pan. Add enough hot milk to reach three-quarters of the way up the pork.

Bring to boil, add lemon rind, then reduce heat. Cover pan, keeping lid slightly askew, and very slowly simmer for about 1.5–2 hours. Resist the temptation to disturb the meat.

When the pork is cooked, milk will have separated and curdled into a golden sauce. Carefully remove meat, slice and serve with sauce spooned over.

THE LEMON IS A BRILLIANT FRUIT.

WITH A LITTLE IMAGINATION,

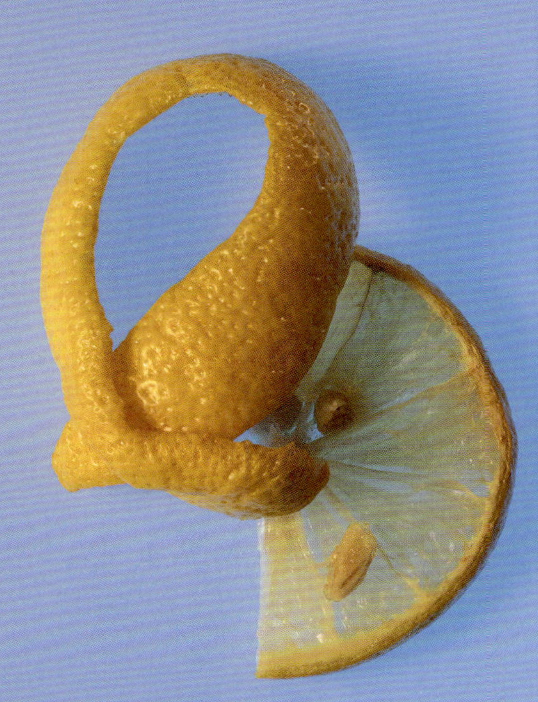

IT CAN BE USED IN INNUMERABLE WAYS.

MAYBE

A TWIST OF LEMON

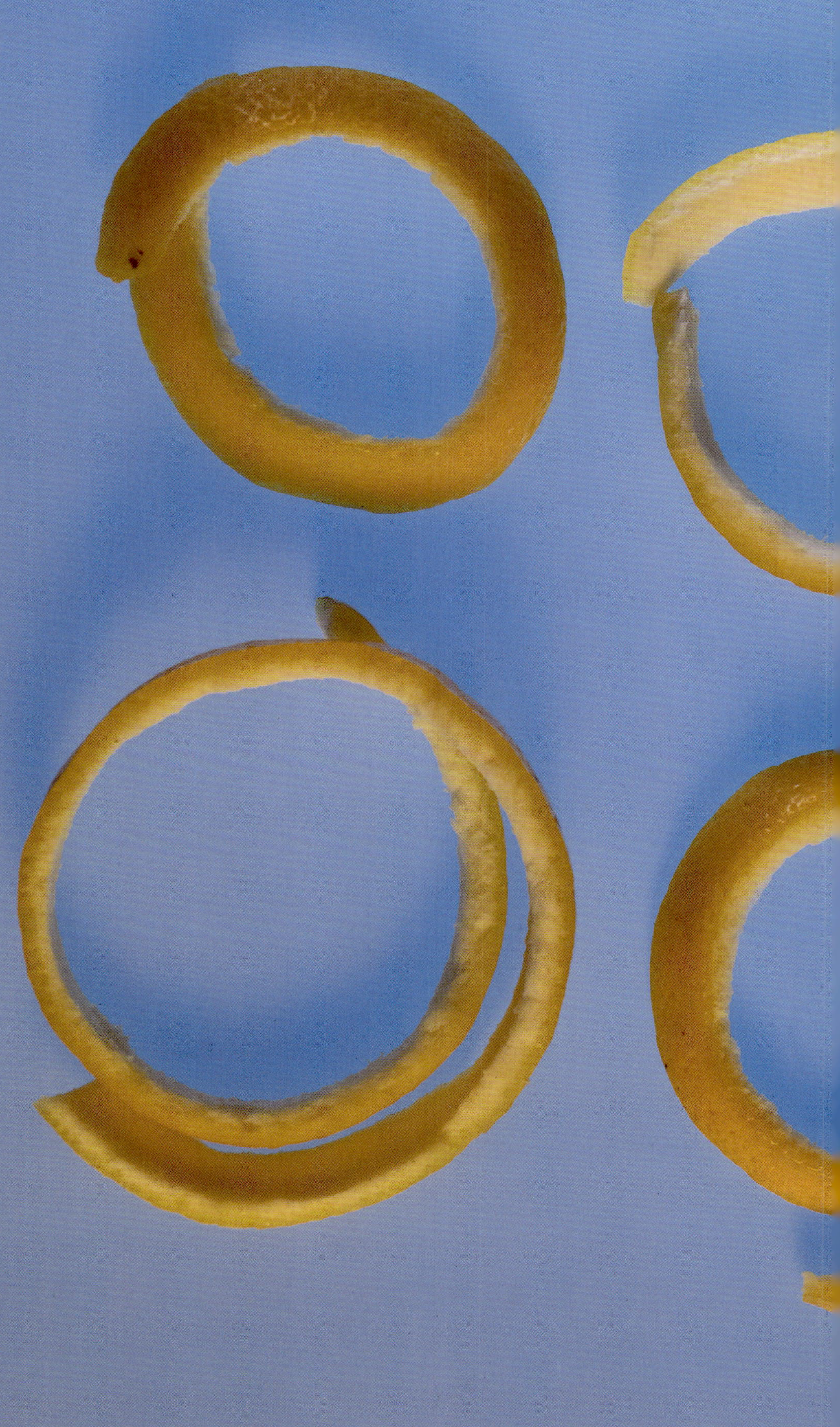

WOULD HELP THIS, OR A SHOT OF WORCESTERSHIRE.

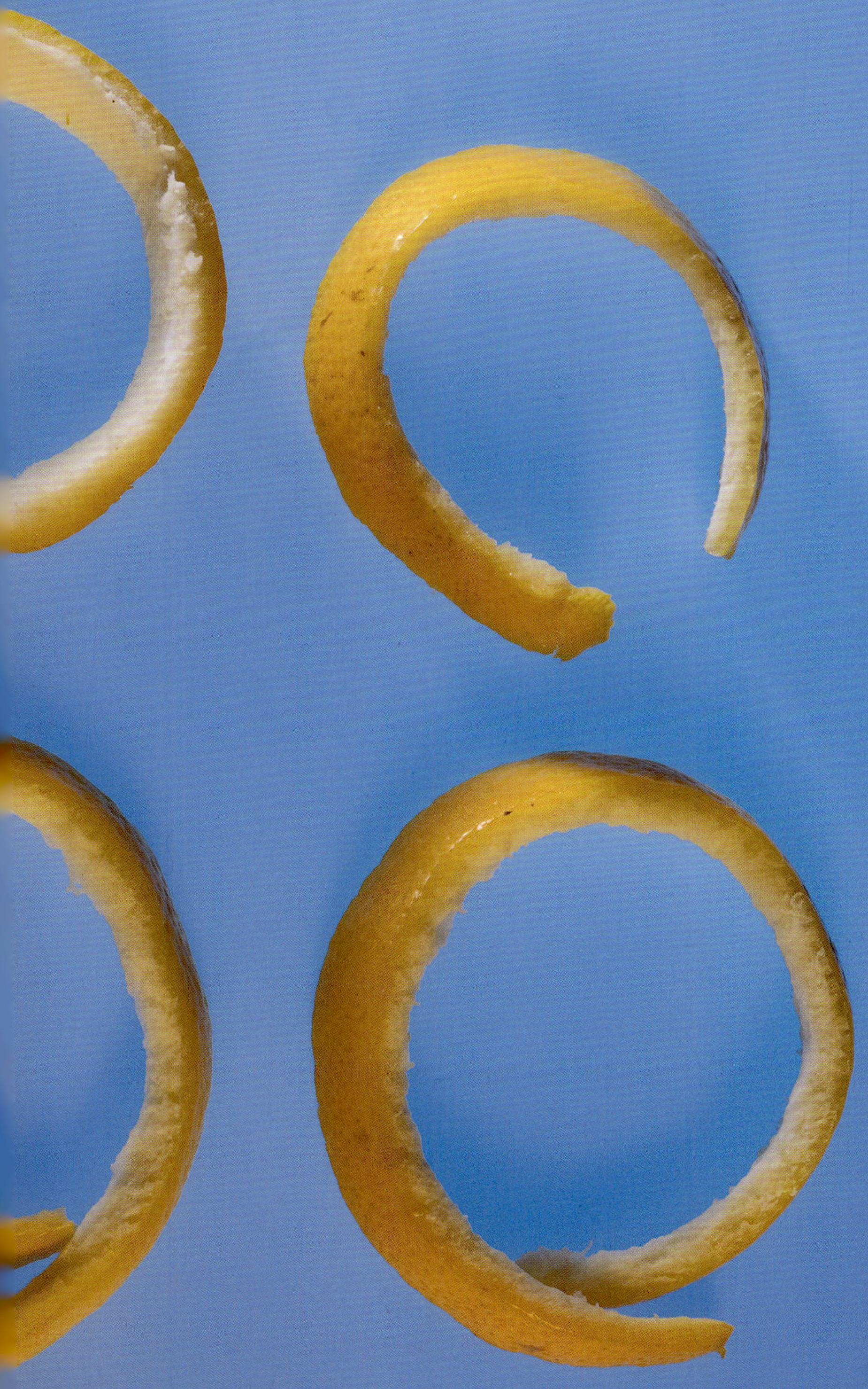

FROM "THE SEVEN YEAR ITC

Raw artichoke salad with lemon

- 4 small globe artichokes with stalks
- Juice of 1 lemon, plus lemon wedges for serving
- Extra virgin olive oil
- Sea salt and freshly ground black pepper
- 1 tender stalk celery, trimmed and finely sliced
- 5¼ ounces Parmesan, very thinly shaved

Remove artichokes' tough outer leaves, leaving paler center leaves; cut off the tops and peel the stalks and hearts. Cut each artichoke in half, and scoop out any choke or bristly purple leaves.

Cut the artichoke hearts as finely as you can, one at a time, placing slices into a bowl and immediately tossing with lemon juice and olive oil. Season with salt and pepper.

Finely slice celery heart, and toss through dressed artichoke. Place on serving plates and cover with Parmesan shavings. Serve drizzled with more olive oil and accompanied by lemon wedges.

Ricciarelli

- 2 to 3 egg whites
- Juice of 1 lemon
- 1¾ cups confectioners' sugar, plus extra for rolling
- 4⅓ cups ground almonds
- Finely grated zest of 2 oranges

Whisk egg whites with lemon juice until soft peaks form. Gradually whisk in confectioners' sugar until mixture is shiny and stiff. Gently fold in ground almonds, salt, and orange zest.

Chill dough in refrigerator for 30 minutes. Preheat oven to 325°.

Generously dust work surface with confectioners' sugar. Roll handful of dough into soft cylinder, 2 inches in diameter. Cut into ½-inch thick slices and roll in more confectioners' sugar. Repeat for remaining dough.

Place biscuits on baking sheet lined with parchment. Bake for 20 minutes.

Risotto with clams, fennel, and lemon

Clams:
- 3 pounds clams, washed
- 2 tablespoons extra virgin olive oil
- 2 garlic cloves, peeled and chopped
- ¾ cup Pinot Bianco

Risotto:
- 6¼ cups fish stock
- 2 tablespoons butter, plus 2 tablespoons cold butter, cubed
- 1 small fennel bulb, chopped, fronds reserved
- 1 clove garlic, peeled and finely chopped
- 1¾ cups carnaroli rice
- ⅔ cup Pinot Bianco
- Juice of 2 lemons

Check over the clams and discard any that are not closed.

In wide pan, heat 2 tablespoons olive oil. Add garlic and cook gently until just soft. Add clams, stir to coat, then add wine. Cover pan and cook over high heat until the clams have opened. When clams are cooked, remove from heat and chill quickly. Remove clams from shells, discarding any that have not opened. Sieve cooking liquor and pour over picked clams.

Heat fish stock to simmer.

Melt 1 tablespoon butter in thick-bottomed pan. Add garlic and chopped fennel, cook for 5 minutes, then add rice and stir to coat each grain. Add wine, and continue stirring as it boils and evaporates. Add stock one ladleful at a time, only adding more when the previous ladleful has been absorbed.

Continue adding stock until rice is al dente. During the last minutes add the clams and their juices. Remove pan from heat and stir in the fennel tops and cold butter, and lemon juice.

Roast guinea fowl stuffed with lemon

- 1 (2 ½-pound) guinea fowl
- Sea salt and freshly ground black pepper
- 2 large lemons
- Fresh bay leaves
- Extra virgin olive oil

Bring guinea fowl to room temperature, and preheat oven to 400°.

Wipe the inside of the guinea fowl with kitchen paper and remove any excess fat from cavity. Season with salt and pepper.

Take the lemons and roll them on a board, using the palm of your hand, pressing down hard to completely soften them, keeping the skin intact. Cut each lemon in half. Tear up the bay leaves.

Push one lemon half and half the bay leaves into the cavity, then insert another lemon half and the rest of the bay leaves. Rub skin of guinea fowl all over with one of the remaining lemon halves and sprinkle with sea salt.

Place bird breast side down in a small high-sided roasting tray. Squeeze over juice of remaining lemon half and drizzle generously with olive oil. Add the squeezed lemons to the tray. Loosely cover with foil. Roast in the oven for 40 minutes.

Remove foil, turn bird over, and roast an additional 30 minutes, or until legs pull away from body and juices are clear.

Leave the guinea fowl to rest for 15 minutes before carving. Serve with lemony roasting juices spooned over.

HEY! DON’T BUY THAT CAR . . .

IT MIGHT BE A LEMON!

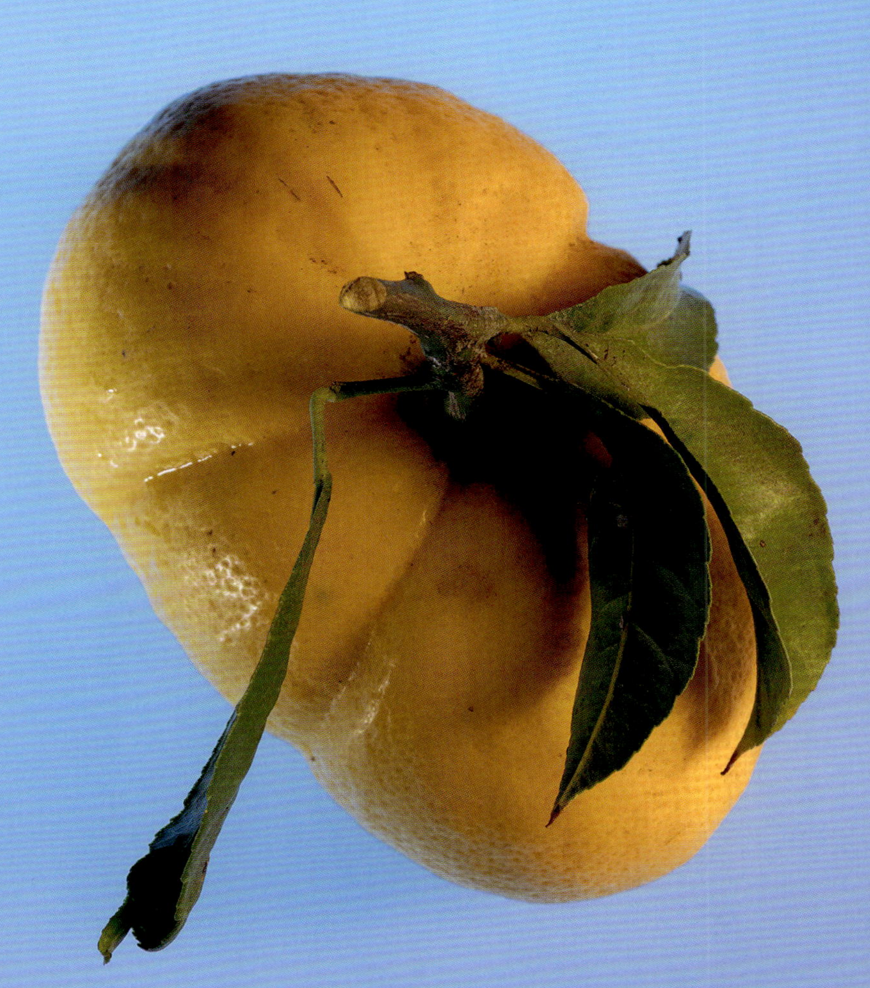

OLD USED CAR ADAGE

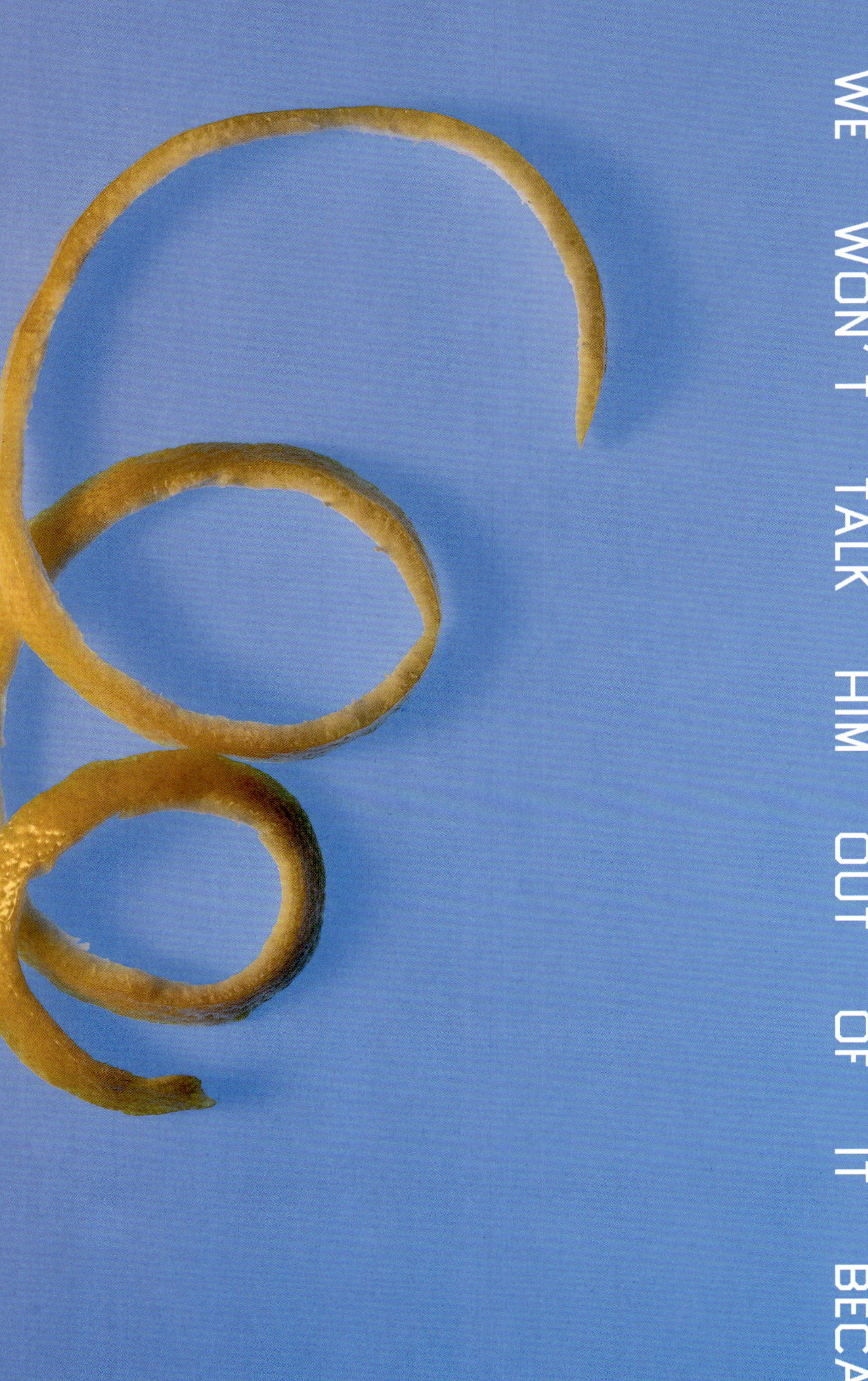
OUR BROTHER THINKS HE'S A LEMON TREE
BUT WE WON'T TALK HIM OUT OF IT BECAUSE
WE NEED THE LEMONS.
APOLOGIES TO GROUCHO MARX

Roast potatoes and lemons

- 2 lemons
- 1½ pounds waxy potatoes, scrubbed and quartered lengthwise
- 4 garlic cloves, halved lengthwise
- 3 tablespoons chopped marjoram leaves
- Sea salt and freshly ground black pepper
- ¼ cup extra virgin olive oil

Preheat the oven to 425°.

Halve the lemons lengthwise, cut each half into three lengthwise wedges, then cut each wedge in half crosswise.

Put the potatoes and lemons into a large bowl. Squeeze the lemons, then add the garlic and marjoram, and season with sea salt and pepper. Add the olive oil and toss to coat evenly.

Place in an ovenproof dish. Roast for 30 minutes, turning the potatoes and lemons regularly so that they are brown and crisp on all sides.

Sea bass carpaccio with lemon and tomato

- 1 (5½-pound) sea bass, scaled, filleted, and deboned
- 8 cherry tomatoes, halved
- Juice of 2 lemons, plus wedges for serving
- Sea salt and freshly ground black pepper
- 3 dried red chilies, ground
- Extra virgin olive oil
- 3 tablespoons chopped marjoram leaves

Place bass fillets skin-side down on chopping board. Using a long-bladed knife, cut into slices as finely as you can along entire length of fillet. Arrange slices side by side on cold plates.

Squeeze tomatoes' juice and some pulp out over the bass. The tomato acids will 'cook' the fish. Drizzle with lemon juice, season and add a few flakes of chili.

Drizzle with olive oil and scatter with marjoram leaves. Serve with lemon wedges.

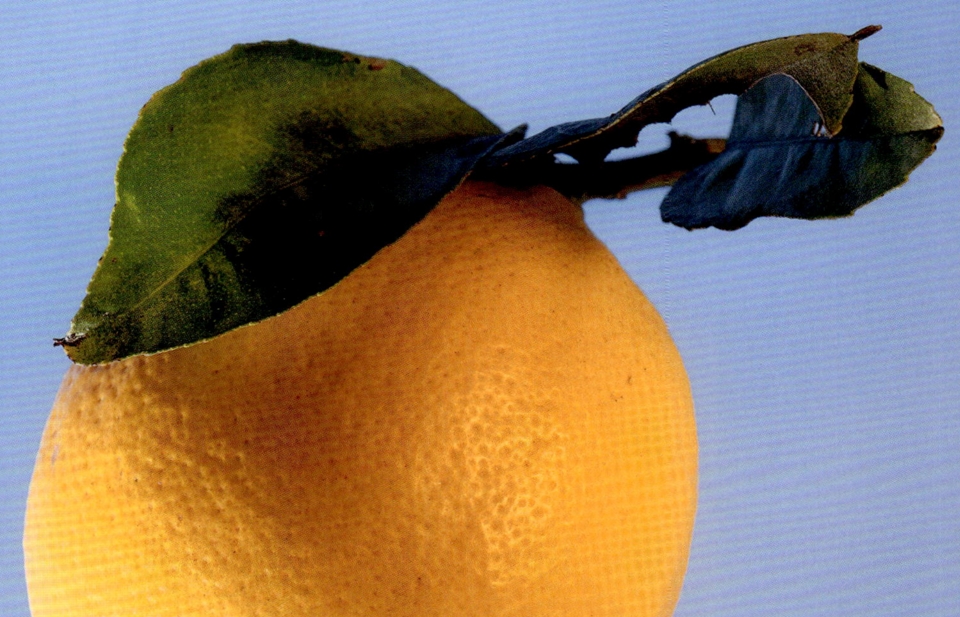

THE LEMON IS SWEET ON THE LIPS
IF TASTED IN TENTATIVE SIPS
IT'S REALLY DELISH
IF SQUEEZED OVER FISH
AND EATEN WITH GREEN PEAS AND FRIES

Spaghetti with garlic, chili, parsley, and lemon

- Sea salt
- Extra virgin olive oil
- 6 garlic cloves, finely sliced
- ¼ cup chopped flat-leaf parsley
- 3 dried red chilies, ground
- Freshly ground black pepper
- Juice of 1 lemon
- 12 ounces spaghetti

Heat splash of olive oil gently in a thick-bottomed pan. Add garlic and fry until soft and golden, then add the parsley and chili. Season to taste, and stir in lemon juice.Cook spaghetti in boiling salted water until al dente. Drain and add to pan of garlic sauce. Toss to combine.

Spaghetti with lemon

- Zest and juice of 2 lemons
- 7 ounces Parmesan, freshly grated, plus more for serving
- Extra virgin olive oil
- Freshly ground black pepper
- 12 ounces spaghetti

Combine lemon juice, zest, and Parmesan, then gradually stir in enough olive oil to make a thick creamy sauce. Season and taste, adding more oil if the sauce is too tart.

Cook spaghetti in boiling salted water until al dente. Drain, keeping back 2 tablespoons cooking water. Return spaghetti and reserved cooking water to the pan. Stir in lemon sauce and add basil, tossing to combine well and coat each strand. Serve with extra Parmesan.

WHEN LIFE HANDS YOU A LEMON, SAY, "OH YEAH, I LIKE LEMONS! WHAT ELSE YA GOT?"

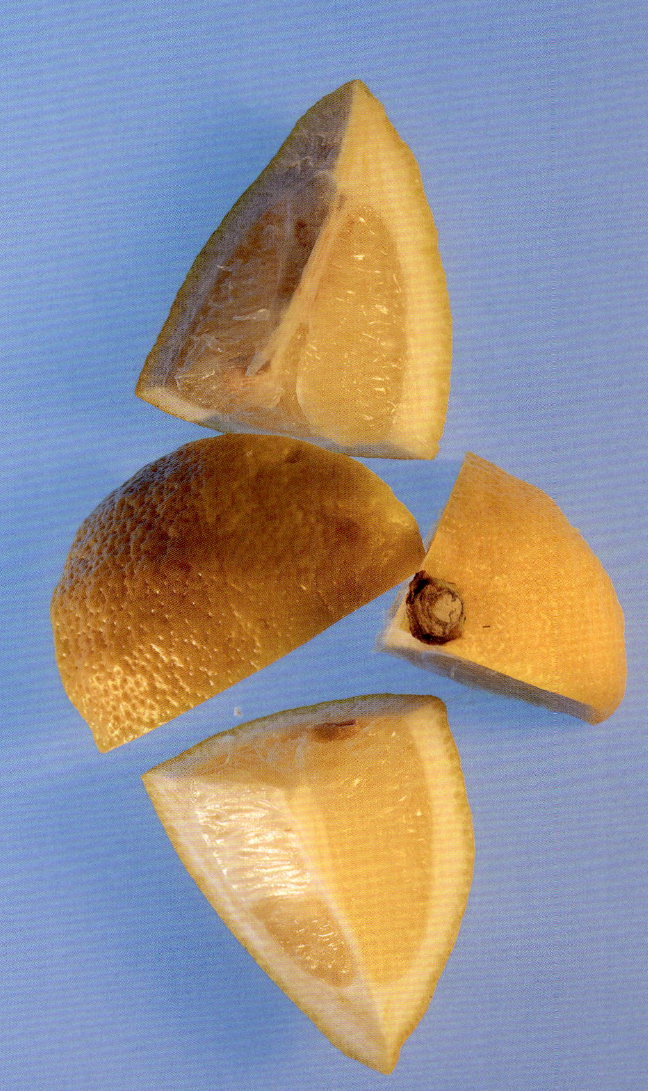

HENRY ROLLINS
MUSICIAN, SPOKEN WORD ARTIST
AND MORE

PEEL PRESERVE PULP

ZEST JUICE

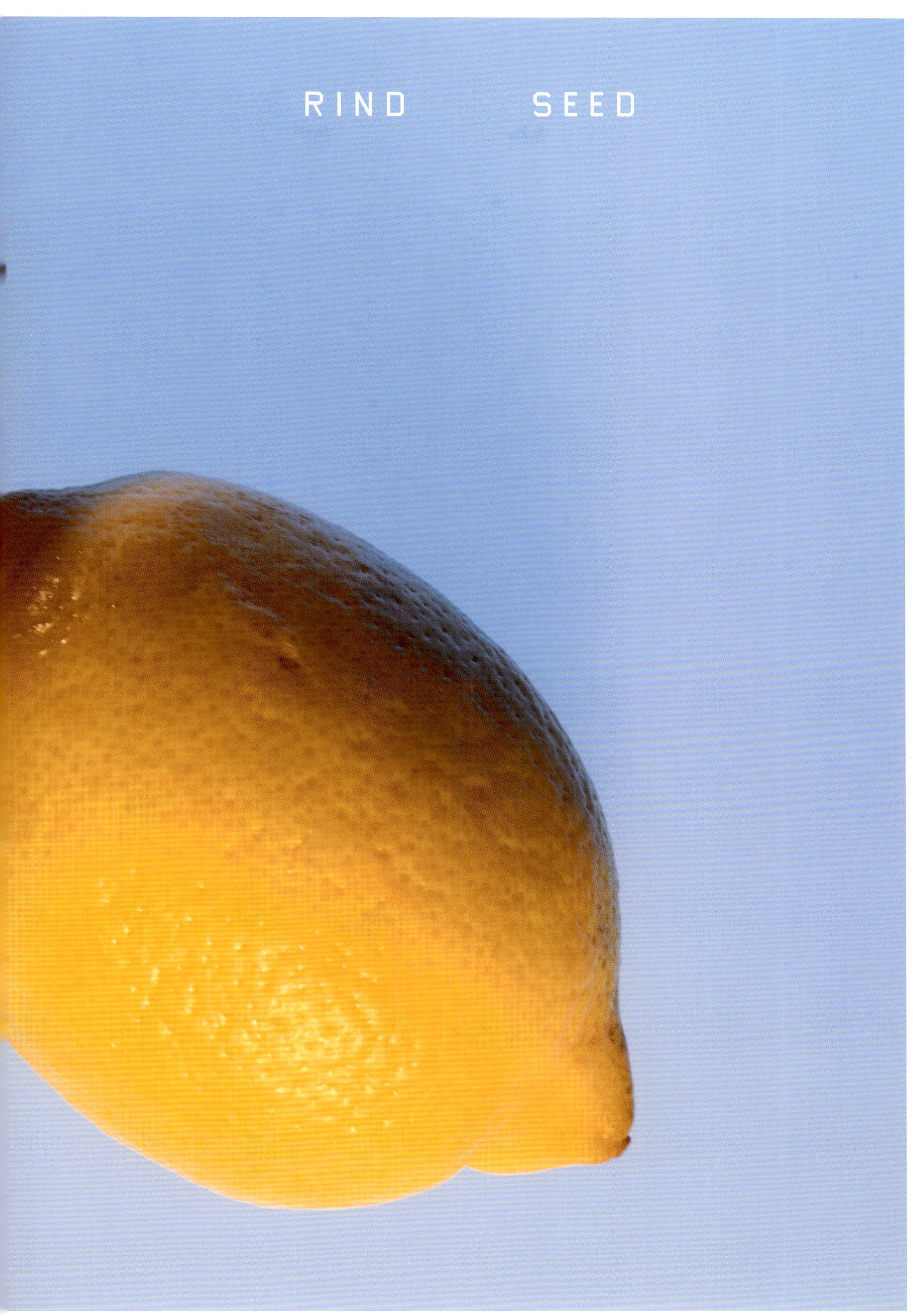
RIND SEED

Spinach with oil and lemon

- 3 tablespoons extra virgin olive oil
- 2 pounds spinach, washed and wet, tough stalks removed
- Sea salt and freshly ground black pepper
- Juice of 1 lemon

Heat oil in a large saucepan with a lid. Add wet spinach, and season with salt and pepper. Stir once, then cover tightly with lid for about a minute, or until spinach is fully wilted. Mix well, add lemon juice, and serve.

YOU HAVE TO SQUEEZE A SONG

FROM ALL SIDES,

LIKE A LEMON.

JOSEPHINE BAKER

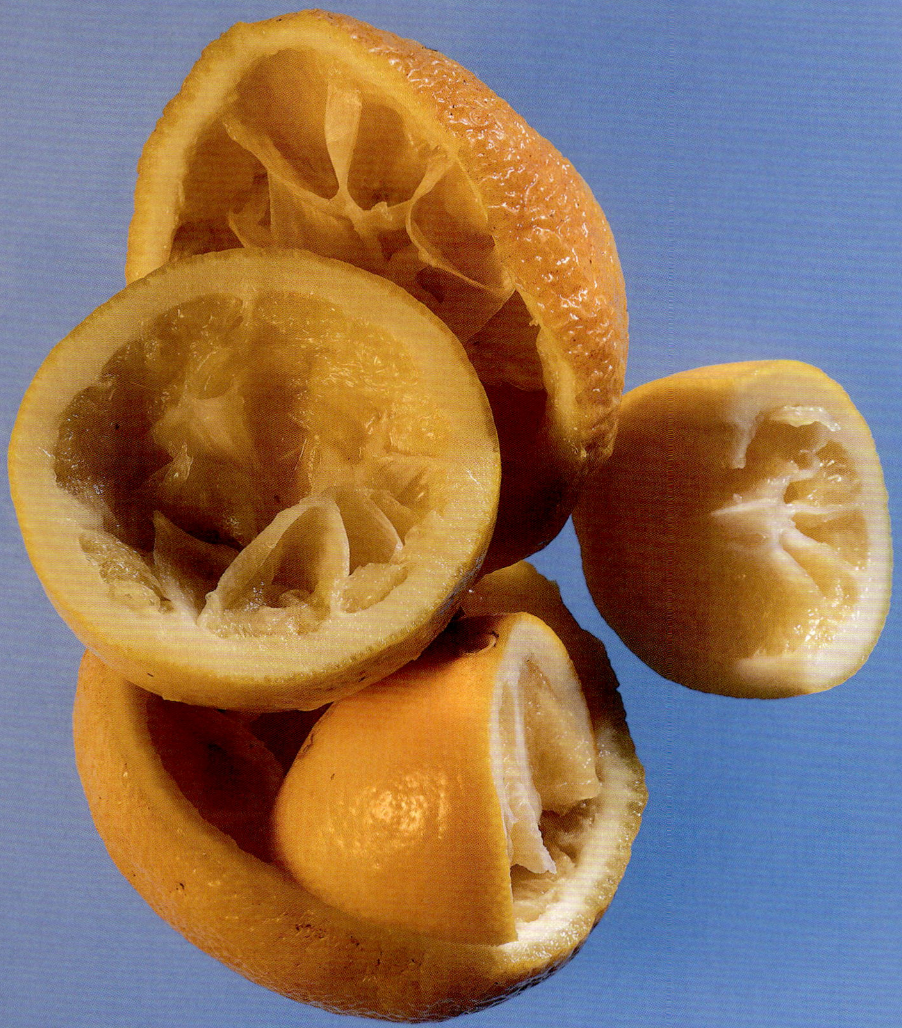

Sweetbread fritto misto with lemon

- 2 pounds sweetbreads
- 4 cups chicken stock
- 2 tablespoons red wine vinegar
- 1 bay leaf
- 1 sprig thyme
- 1 sprig sage, plus leaves from 1 bunch
- 3 cloves garlic
- Sea salt
- 5 quarts sunflower oil
- 1¾ cups semolina flour
- 2½ cups all-purpose flour or pasta flour
- Freshly ground black pepper
- 2 cups whole milk
- ¼ cup salted capers, rinsed
- 2 lemons, cut into wedges

Soak sweetbreads in cold water for a couple of hours to remove any impurities, then drain. Place sweetbreads in a pot with the chicken stock, red wine vinegar, bay leaf, thyme and sage sprigs, garlic, and salt. Bring up to a gentle simmer over a medium heat and simmer for 3–4 minutes. Remove from heat and leave sweetbreads to cool in liquor.

Once sweetbreads are cool, remove them from the liquor and peel away outer membranes.

Heat sunflower oil in a large pot or deep-fat fryer to 350°.

Mix together the semolina and flour and season with sea salt and black pepper. One at a time, dip sweetbreads in milk, then transfer to the flour and turn to coat. Shake off any excess flour.

Gently place dredged sweetbreads into the hot oil and fry until golden brown. Just before you remove sweetbreads from oil, throw in capers and sage leaves. The sage and capers will go crispy.

Drain everything on paper towels. Sprinkle with more sea salt and serve with wedges of lemon.

HE BURST INTO THE ROOM,

F I L L E D

WITH PITH AND VINEGAR.

WHEN LIFE GIVES YOU LIMES,

PRETEND

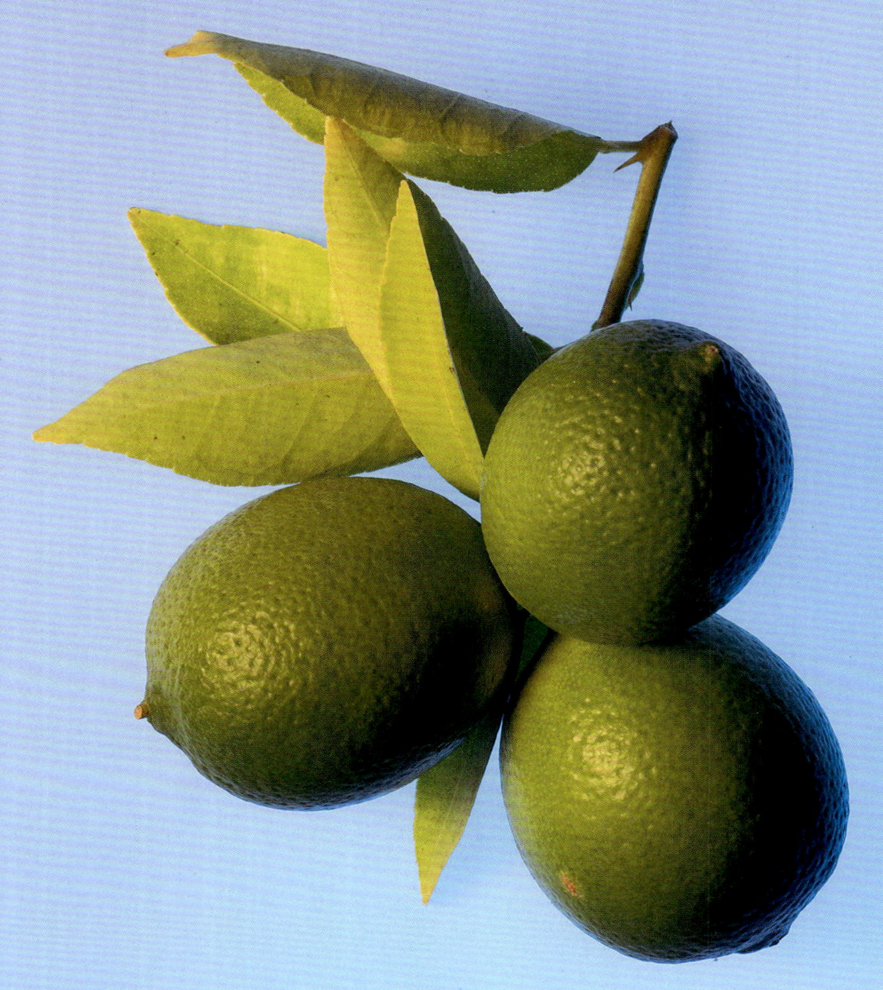

Swiss chard with olive oil and lemon

- Sea salt
- 2 pounds Swiss chard, stalks and leaves separated
- Juice of 1 lemon
- Freshly ground black pepper

Cut each chard stalk into ½-inch thick pieces. Cook the stalks in boiling salted water for 5 minutes or until tender. Remove from the water with a slotted spoon and drain.

In the same pot, cook chard leaves until tender. Drain and roughly chop. Mix with the stalks.

Combine lemon juice with four times its volume of olive oil. Season, pour over chard, and toss well. Serve at room temperature.

Tagliatelle with lemon, cream, and parsley

- 1¼ cups heavy cream
- 1 stick/8 tablespoons unsalted butter, softened
- Zest and juice of 3 organic lemons
- 12 ounces egg tagliatelle
- 3 tablespoons roughly chopped flat-leaf parsley
- 4 ounces Parmesan, freshly grated

Gently heat cream in small thick-bottomed saucepan. When warm, add butter and lemon juice and zest. Stir to combine, then remove from heat.

Cook tagliatelle in boiling salted water until al dente. Drain and stir into the warm cream, seasoning to taste. Add half the parsley and toss well.

Serve with the Parmesan and the remainder of the parsley sprinkled over.

WE ARE LIVING IN A WORLD TODAY WHERE LEMONADE IS MADE WITH ARTIFICIAL FLAVORS AND FURNITURE POLISH IS MADE FROM REAL LEMONS. ALFRED E. NEUMAN

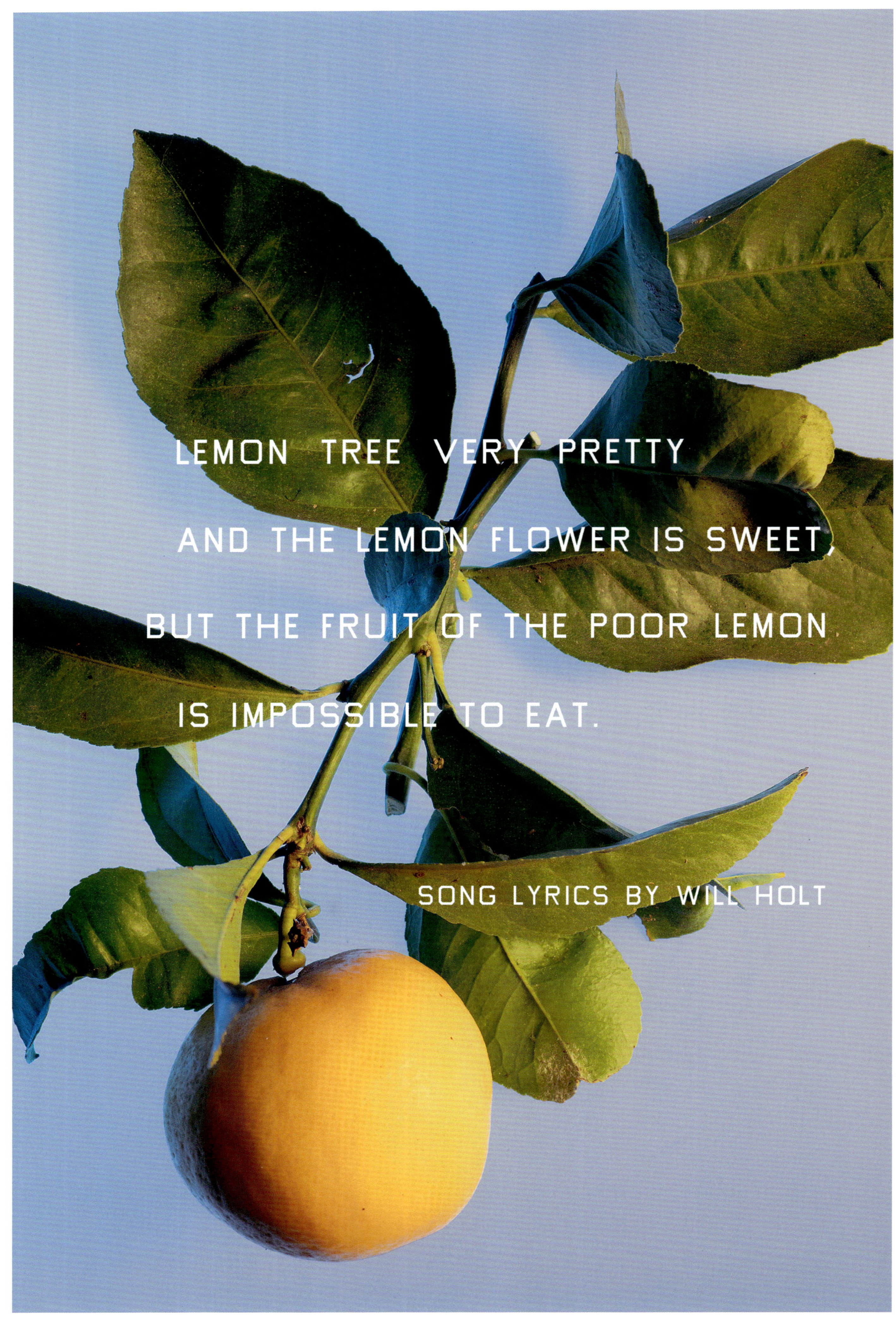
LEMON TREE VERY PRETTY
AND THE LEMON FLOWER IS SWEET,
BUT THE FRUIT OF THE POOR LEMON
IS IMPOSSIBLE TO EAT.
SONG LYRICS BY WILL HOLT

Vegetable and lemon fritto misto

Batter:
- 1¼ cups all-purpose flour
- 3 tablespoons extra virgin olive oil
- 3 egg whites

Vegetables:
- 8 cups sunflower oil
- 8 anchovy fillets
- 16 large sage leaves
- All-purpose flour, for dusting
- 9 ounces zucchini, sliced into ¼-inch discs, then cut into ¼-inch sticks
- Sea salt
- 8 zucchini flowers, stamens and sepals removed
- 1 eggplant, sliced into ¼-inch discs
- 2 lemons, thinly sliced, plus 2 lemons, cut into wedges for serving

Make batter: sieve flour into a medium bowl, and make well in centre. Pour in olive oil, and stir to gradually combine flour and oil. And stir slowly combining the flour into the oil. Loosen this paste with warm water, added slowly, stirring constantly, until batter is consistency of double cream. Let stand minimum 45 minutes.

Place an anchovy fillet between 2 sage leaves and press to hold together. The oiliness of the anchovy will help the sage to stick. Dust with plain flour. Repeat with remaining anchovies and sage.

In high-sided pan, heat sunflower oil to 350°. Beat egg whites until stiff, and fold into batter.

Dip zucchini, eggplant, flowers, and lemons in batter, tapping to gently remove excess. Fry in batches until golden brown and crisp. Drain onto kitchen paper.

Fry anchovy and sage directly in oil without any batter. Serve a selection, seasoned with sea salt and a wedge of lemon.

LEMONS ARE SOUR.

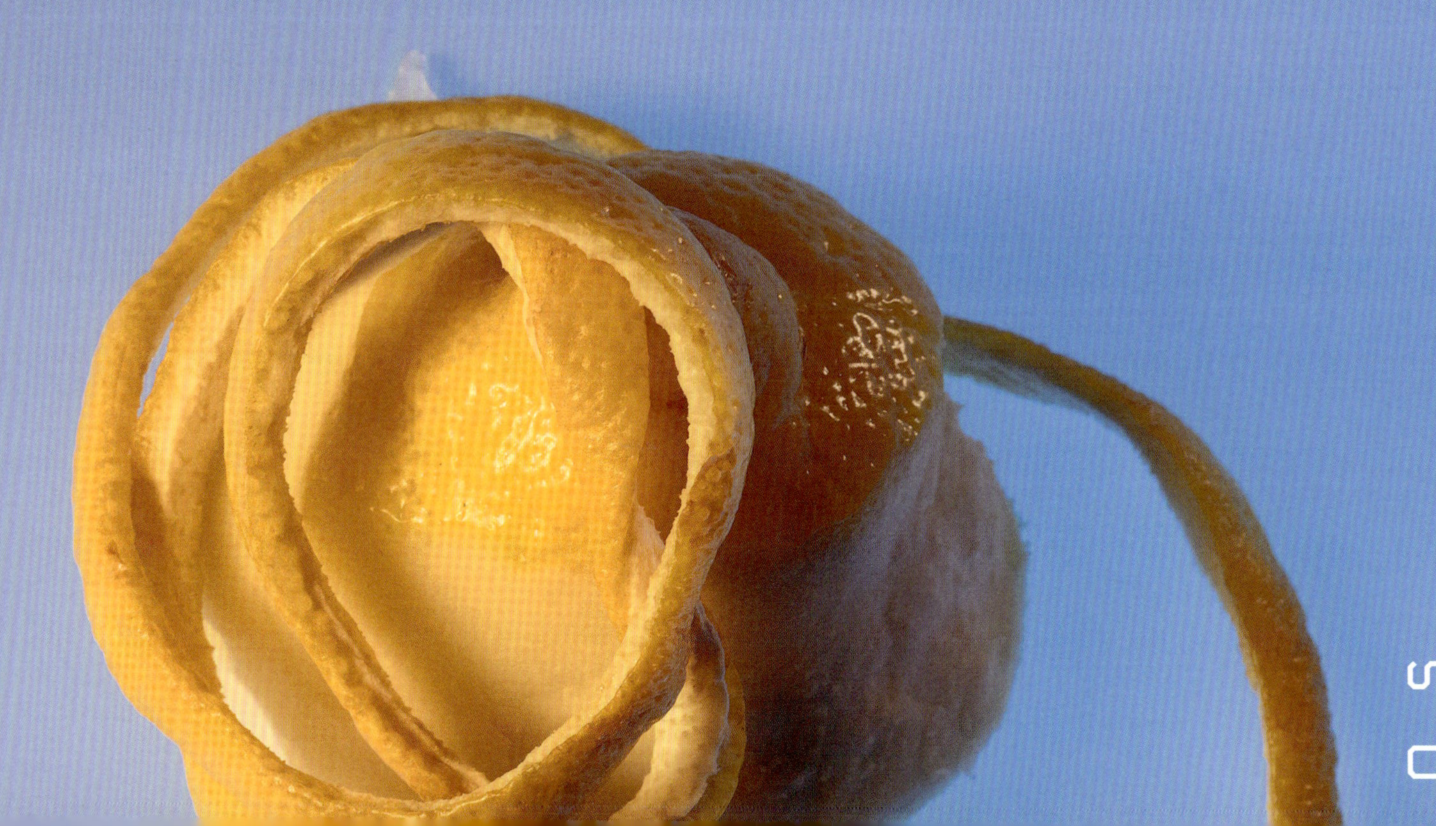

SO WHAT!

WHAT?

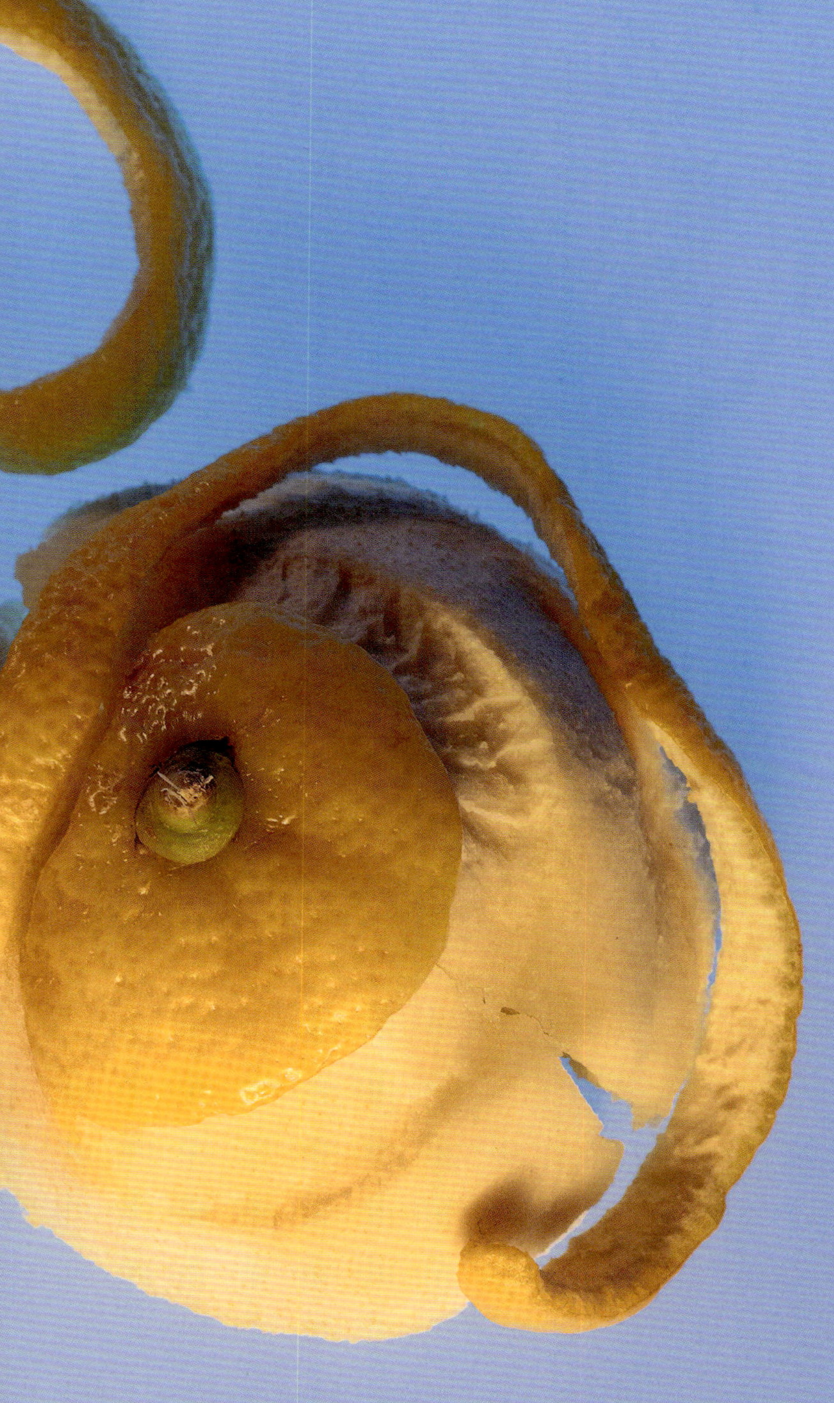

LEMONS ARE ESSENTIAL.

THAT'S

Whiskey Sour

- 2½ fluid ounces Scotch whiskey (Lagavulin or Glenfiddich)
- ⅛ fluid ounce sugar syrup
- 1 fluid ounce lemon juice
- ¾ fluid ounce egg white
- 3 dashes Angostura bitters

Pour whiskey, lemon juice, egg white, and sugar syrup into cocktail shaker. Cover and shake well without ice to emulsify egg white.

Open shaker, fill with ice, close again, and shake until thoroughly chilled.

Strain into cocktail glass filled with fresh cubed ice.

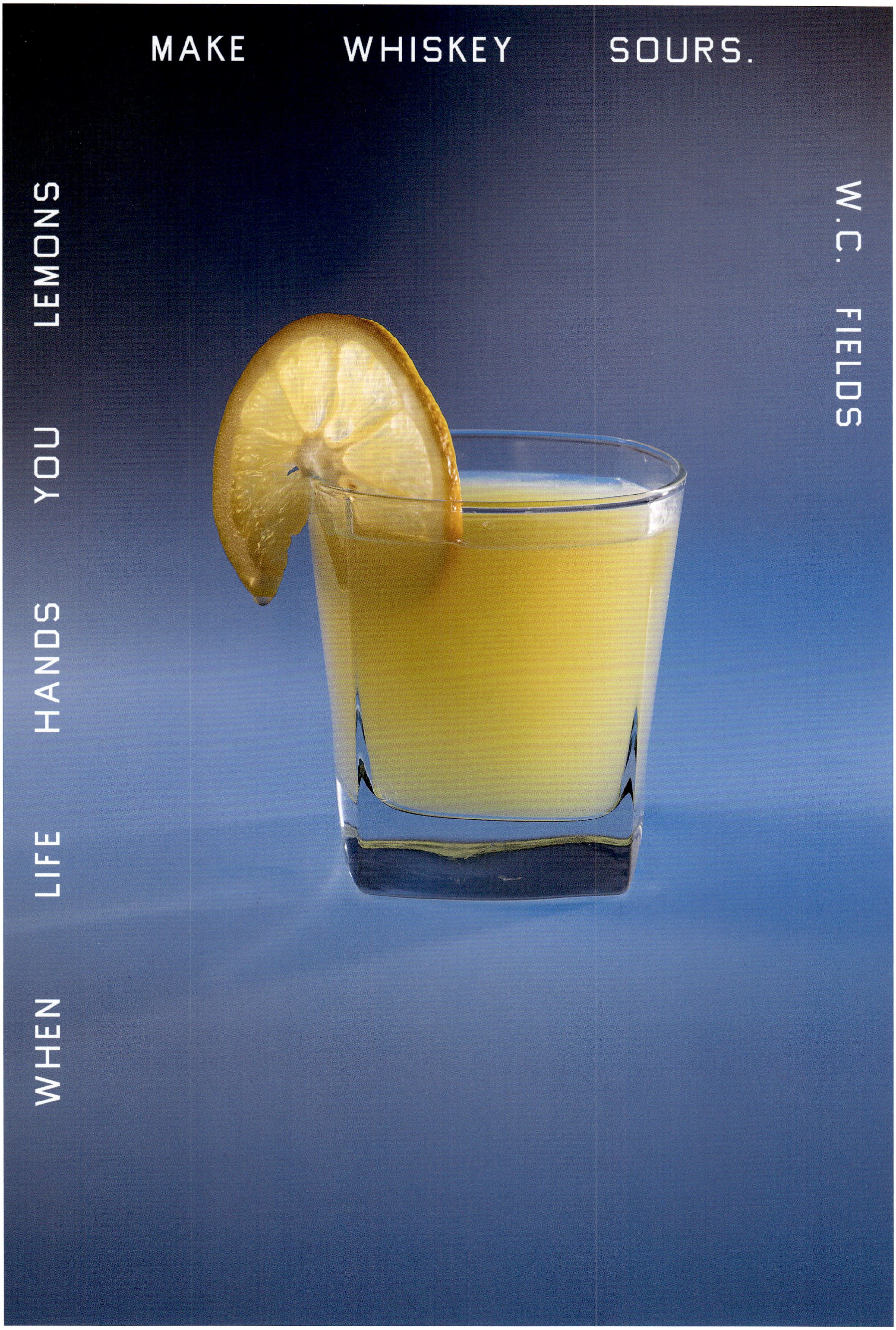

WHEN LIFE HANDS YOU LEMONS

MAKE WHISKEY SOURS.

W.C. FIELDS

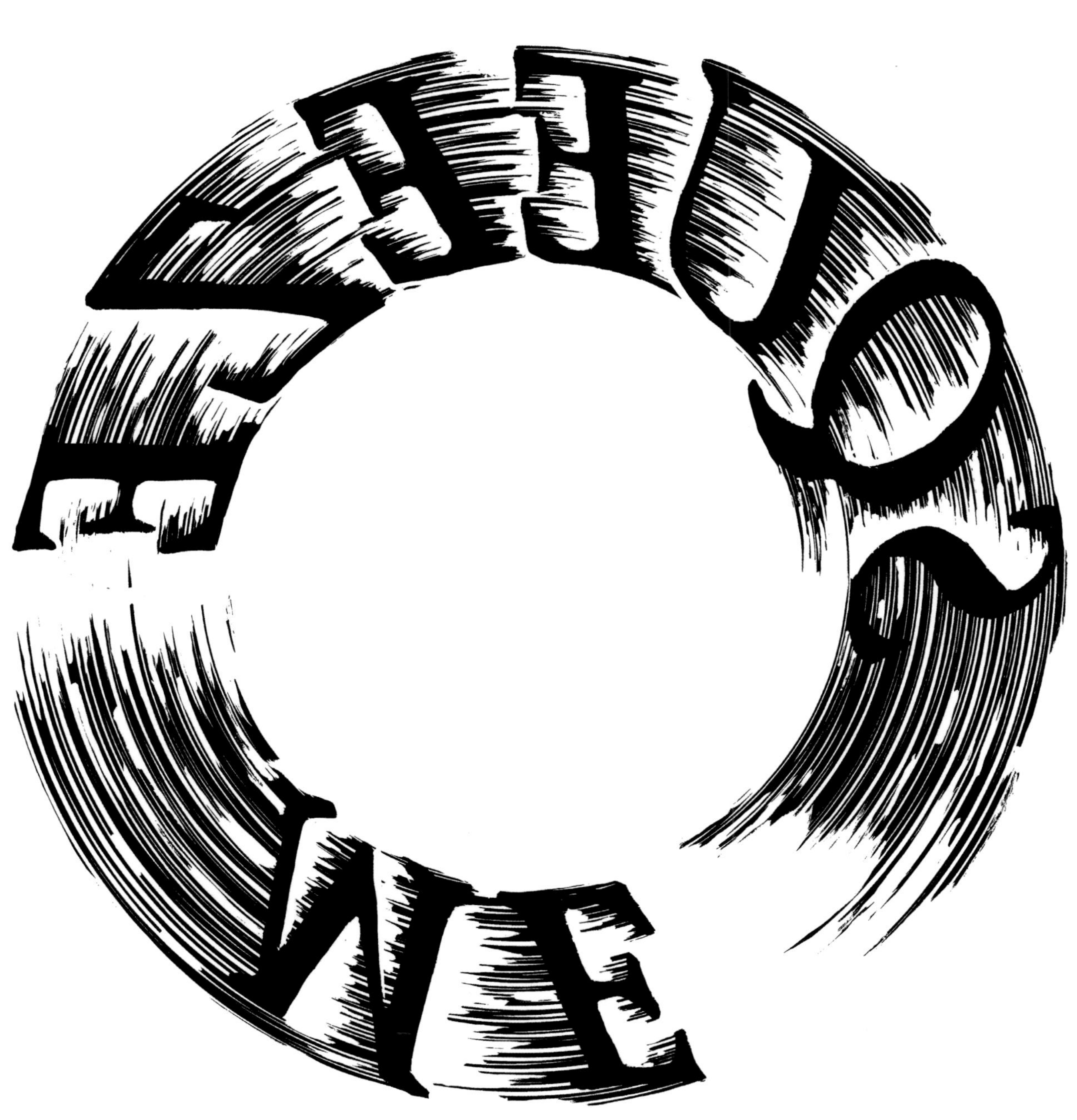

Acknowledgments

Kitty Alford
Vashti Armit
Antonio Cavedoni
Mary Dean
Giulia Di Filippo
Matthew Donaldson
Roger Guyett
Susan Haller
Jemima Kiss
Jude Marwa
Caroline Michel
Charles Miers
Sian Wyn Owen
Charles Pullan
Nina Raine
Gary Regester
Roo Rogers
Ed Ruscha Studio
Ella Shindler
Maude Tisch
Joseph Trivelli
Chris Wilson

First published in the United States of America
in 2025 by Rizzoli International Publications, Inc.
49 West 27th Street
New York, NY 10001
www.rizzoliusa.com

For Rizzoli International Publications, Inc.
Publisher: Charles Miers
Senior Editor: Giulia Di Filippo
Production Manager: Kaija Markoe
Managing Editor: Lynn Scrabis

Book Design by LoveFrom

This book has been typeset in LoveFrom Sans

ISBN: 978-0-8478-7593-1
A Library of Congress Control Number
is available upon request.

Printed in Italy
2026 2027 2028 2029 / 10 9 8 7 6 5 4

The authorized representative in the
EU for product safety and compliance is
Mondadori Libri S.p.A.
via Gian Battista Vico 42
Milan 20123
Italy
www.mondadori.it

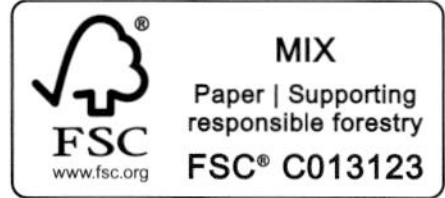

Visit us online:
Instagram.com/RizzoliBooks
Facebook.com/RizzoliNewYork
Youtube.com/user/RizzoliNY

"Yeah I love these lemons...
I can eat these just as they are."

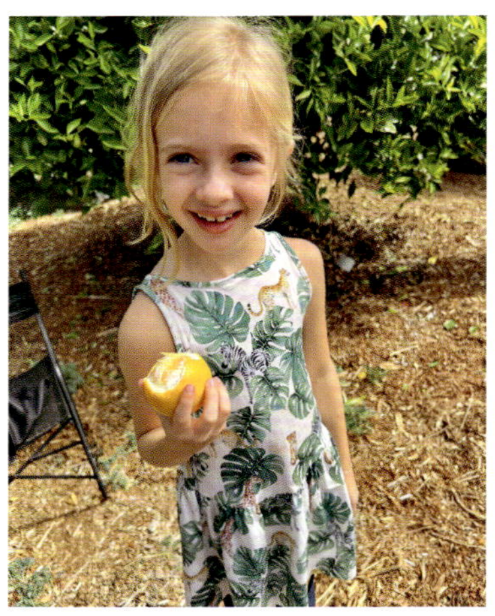

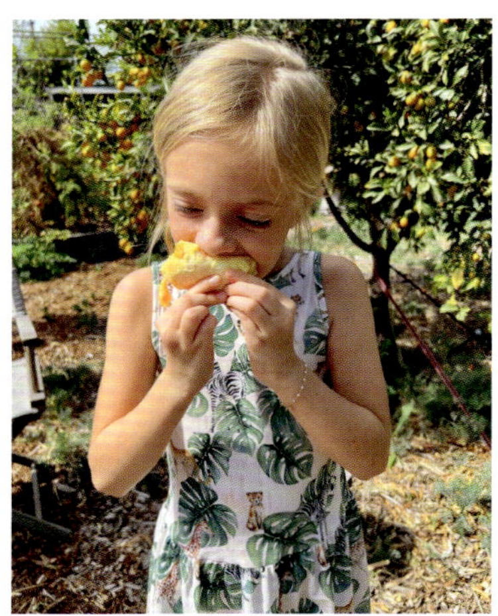

Frankie Kopelman photographed by
Will Kopelman at Ed's studio, March 2022.